COMPASSIONATE
ACCOUNTABILITY

COMPASSIONATE
ACCOUNTABILITY

How Leaders Build Connection and Get Results

NATE REGIER, PHD

Berrett–Koehler Publishers, Inc.

The rights for the images on pages 7, 127, 159 were acquired from Depositphotos. The images on pages 17, 18, 41, 44, 55, 83, 99 were designed by Scott Light, CG Studios.

Berrett-Koehler Publishers, Inc.
1333 Broadway, Suite 1000
Oakland, CA 94612-1921
Tel: (510) 817-2277
Fax: (510) 817-2278
www.bkconnection.com

ORDERING INFORMATION

Quantity sales. Special discounts are available on quantity purchases by corporations, associations, and others. For details, contact the "Special Sales Department" at the Berrett-Koehler address above.

Individual sales. Berrett-Koehler publications are available through most bookstores. They can also be ordered directly from Berrett-Koehler: Tel: (800) 929-2929; Fax: (802) 864-7626; www.bkconnection .com.

Orders for college textbook / course adoption use. Please contact Berrett-Koehler: Tel: (800) 929-2929; Fax: (802) 864-7626.

Distributed to the US trade and internationally by Penguin Random House Publisher Services.

Berrett-Koehler and the BK logo are registered trademarks of Berrett-Koehler Publishers, Inc.

Printed in the United States of America

Berrett-Koehler books are printed on long-lasting acid-free paper. When it is available, we choose paper that has been manufactured by environmentally responsible processes. These may include using trees grown in sustainable forests, incorporating recycled paper, minimizing chlorine in bleaching, or recycling the energy produced at the paper mill.

Library of Congress Cataloging-in-Publication Data

Names: Regier, Nate, author.
Title: Compassionate accountability : how leaders build connection and get
  results / Nate Regier, PhD.
Description: First edition. | Oakland, CA : Berrett-Koehler Publishers,
  [2023] | Includes bibliographical references and index.
Identifiers: LCCN 2022058282 (print) | LCCN 2022058283 (ebook) | ISBN
  9781523004539 (paperback) | ISBN 9781523004546 (pdf) | ISBN
  9781523004553 (epub) | ISBN 9781523004560 (audio)
Subjects: LCSH: Compassion. | Responsibility. | Leadership. | Management.
Classification: LCC BJ1475 .R44 2023 (print) | LCC BJ1475 (ebook) | DDC
  177/.7—dc23/eng/20230201
LC record available at https://lccn.loc.gov/2022058282
LC ebook record available at https://lccn.loc.gov/2022058283

First Edition
30 29 28 27 26 25 24 23   10 9 8 7 6 5 4 3 2 1

Book producer: PeopleSpeak
Text designer: Reider Books
Cover designer: Adam Johnson

Compassionate Accountability is a mindset, philosophy, and way of living that we've evolved at Next Element thanks to the influence of people who reject the notion that these two concepts are in opposition.

If you are the kind of leader who looks for a third way and believes that conflict has the potential to create a better world, you are an antidote to drama. This book is dedicated to you.

If you are at an organization that strives for excellence through the power of relationships, you are making a huge difference in the world. This book is dedicated to you.

If you are a change maker who won't compromise the dignity of another human being while holding them accountable for their behavior, you are a catalyst for a better world. This book is dedicated to you.

Compassion is what makes us human, brings us together, and gets us back on track when we lose our way. If you strive to embody and live this kind of compassion, this book is dedicated to you.

"Compassion is an action word with no boundaries."

—*Prince*

CONTENTS

Part IV: Overcoming Barriers to Compassion

FOREWORD

AS AN EXECUTIVE COACH for over forty years, I have made it my goal to help great leaders get even better. As my clients know, what I teach is easy to understand yet difficult to do. Change is hard! We know that our habits, lifestyles, and leadership behaviors hold us back from being able to get better, but we still fall back into the same patterns time and again.

Compassionate Accountability is the leadership standard of the future. It requires that leaders be engaged and intentional about their interactions with their teams and the behaviors that impact them. This strikes at the heart of positive, lasting change—combining accountability and repeated follow-up, while building trust and vulnerability within the team.

The core of my coaching throughout my career has been a process I call *stakeholder-centered coaching*. This starts with an interview with all the leader's stakeholders: direct reports, colleagues, superiors, and board members, as well as friends and family around the leader that can speak to their leadership style and impacts from different angles. After these confidential discussions, I then review with the leader the high-level takeaways for their leadership in both the positives and areas for improvement. At this meeting, we talk about what the leader wants to improve and, consequently, what they'll be working on with me for the length of their coaching contract.

And then they're done. We don't talk to the group of people again or involve them now that we've gotten their feedback, right?

Wrong!

The whole point of this process is that these people are *stakeholders* and have a stake in the leader's growth and progress. The change a leader makes isn't measured by the leader or myself but instead by the people that experience the leadership every day! The executive brings the stakeholders in as accountability partners and asks on a regularly scheduled basis for ideas and suggestions for the future on their chosen areas for improvement.

This builds enormous trust within the team as they see the leader's humility to ask for help and continue to seek their advice about their progress. Leaders need to adopt this type of Compassionate Accountability practice to get better.

Dr. Nate Regier has created an expertly written and researched guide to harnessing Compassionate Accountability and using it to improve your teams, organization, and life. The book flows thoughtfully as it talks about compassion in this context, the place it holds in business, and the barriers surrounding it. With actionable steps and packed with real-world examples of its effects, this book will give you the tools you need to start implementing these new behaviors right away.

My advice is to read this book, take its advice, and watch the way it transforms your team and business.

—Dr. Marshall Goldsmith, *Thinkers50* #1 Executive Coach
and *New York Times* bestselling author or coauthor of
The Earned Life, Triggers, and *What Got
You Here Won't Get You There*

INTRODUCTION

EVERY LEADER faces the same conundrum many times a day, a dilemma that pulls them in opposite directions where neither direction is sustainable or ultimately effective. Every day they crave a way to reconcile these opposites and too often find themselves either choosing sides in a desperate attempt to find an anchor in the storm or vacillating between extremes to soothe their ambivalence.

The conundrum is to reconcile compassion with accountability.

I've heard this conundrum expressed in many ways:

- People versus tasks
- Process versus content
- Relationships versus results
- Peace versus justice

I've intentionally used *versus* to juxtapose these pairs of words and underscore the shared experience of so many leaders we work with— the perception that these priorities are in opposition or tension with each other.

Regardless of how you frame it, we all face this challenge. People tend toward one dimension of these pairs or the other, but nobody can be fully effective as a leader without doing both well.

Choosing one side over the other has predictably negative results. On one hand, compassion without accountability gets you nowhere.

Results suffer. On the other hand, accountability without compassion gets you alienated. Connection suffers.

Vacillating between extremes also has negative consequences, leaving a leader feeling unsure and incompetent while their followers experience them as inconsistent, unpredictable, and fickle.

It doesn't have to be this way. The solution is Compassionate Accountability. Embracing both without compromising either is not only possible but also transformative for individuals, relationships, teams, and work cultures. To get there, we need to reimagine our understanding and practice of compassion as leaders.

What's Inside

This book is assembled in four parts, each a piece of the Compassionate Accountability puzzle.

In part 1, "The Big Idea," you will learn the background and argument for why Compassionate Accountability is both revolutionary and required for the world of work and beyond. In chapter 1, "The Evolution of Compassion," you will explore how our understanding and practice of compassion has evolved over the years, especially within a corporate work context. You'll see how compassion has been hollowed out, stripped of its power, and misused, especially during times of crisis and disruption. Most of the strife we see in our world and organizations is a result of the artificial dichotomy that puts compassion and accountability in opposition to each other.

The silver lining, and the main premise of this book, is revealed in chapter 2, "Compassion and Accountability Are Complementary," which contains the argument that compassion and accountability are not opposites. In fact, compassion without accountability isn't even compassion. And accountability without compassion is simply inhumane. They can't exist alone and were never meant to.

Right now, in companies around the world, we are seeing an emergence of a more evolved type of compassion that recognizes and includes accountability. Leaders and organizations are currently implementing a cultural revolution that includes all the best of what compassion is, while transcending limiting beliefs and habits that have held us back. Examples of these transformative efforts are sprinkled throughout.

In part 2, "The Model," you will get straight to the practical stuff by learning the mindset and behavioral framework for Compassionate Accountability. In chapter 3, "What Is the Compassion Mindset?", you will explore how Compassionate Accountability starts with a specific mindset, a choice to view ourselves and others differently. The compassion mindset has three switches, each connected to one necessary, but not sufficient, component of Compassionate Accountability. Chapters 4 through 6 each address one of three switches of the compassion mindset. You will learn the harmful but all-too-common leadership behaviors that occur when these switches are turned off. More importantly, you will see detailed examples of the leadership choices and behaviors that turn on each switch and keep it on. Quizzes, self-assessment checklists, tons of examples, and chapter highlights will help bring the concepts down to ground level.

Part 3, "Implementation," is for organizations seeking to make Compassionate Accountability more prevalent in their culture. Chapter 7 is your implementation road map. It starts by summarizing the impact on work culture when the compassion mindset switches are off or on. Next you will get several fundamental principles to follow when implementing this framework in your organization. Learn how the practice of Compassionate Accountability dovetails perfectly with what the next generation of employees wants and needs to stay engaged.

Every journey requires an accurate assessment of where you are and where you want to go. You will get an assessment to evaluate where each of the three switches is positioned for you, among your team, and in your organization. Culture is about behavior norms, so you will also get a detailed guide on how to set and enforce behavior norms around Compassionate Accountability.

You will also receive recommendations on the top six areas to focus on to change your culture. Don't miss the three most important questions you should include in every employee and customer survey.

Chapter 8 contains several case studies of organizations that have embraced the process of transformation with Compassionate Accountability. Learn insights, tips, and strategies that you can use on your journey.

Part 4, "Overcoming Barriers to Compassion," is for anyone who is struggling to get on board. We've worked with thousands of leaders who are trying to reconcile connection with results and want to make the difficult leap to a third way. Along the way we've identified five common misconceptions about compassion that create barriers for people. Each one has to do with how we have learned to view compassion and limits us in some way. Each chapter explores one of these barriers, revealing how it holds us back and offering the research and anecdotes pointing to a new, more healthy, and empowering relationship with compassion. Each chapter ends with a summary of the barrier, the reality, a more hopeful message, and tips for how to apply the new insight.

If you bought into the message of this book and are on board with Compassionate Accountability, feel free to skip this section. If you aren't sure, are struggling with the concepts, or want encouragement, you aren't alone. This part is for you. If you are trying to help someone else reimagine their understanding and practice of compassion, this part might give you some empathy and insights on how to support them in the most helpful way.

This book is full of real examples, stories, and case studies alongside contemporary research and data. All stories and depictions are based on real events, but details and identities may have been changed to protect privacy.

Benefits You Can Experience

Here's some of what you can gain when you read this book and take action on what's inside:

- More confidence to navigate messy, complicated, and challenging situations
- A sense of stability, presence, and centeredness during uncertainty
- Clarity around the attitudes and behaviors that matter most
- Inner peace and sense of purpose
- Greater satisfaction as a leader
- Improved engagement from your employees
- More cohesive, trusting, and higher functioning teams
- Unifying principles, processes, and behaviors for a thriving organization
- Hope that you can make a positive difference, especially in complex and difficult situations

I say this confidently because our global community of leaders who are practicing Compassionate Accountability have seen the results. We have accumulated fifteen years of shared experience in a dozen countries around the world, countless anecdotes of transformation, and over twenty-five thousand data points of outcomes research showing positive change. The experiences of numerous thought leaders, researchers, and change makers are woven in to illustrate and support the transformational potential in Compassionate Accountability.

Caveat: "Tools Don't Work–You Do"

"Tools don't work—you do" might be my favorite nugget of wisdom from my Next Element colleague and cofounder, Jamie Remsberg. Even as I write, my woodworking shop is full of amazing tools capable of creating incredible pieces of carpentry. But right now they sit idly, accomplishing nothing. I guess my tools don't work. But you should see some of the woodwork I've built with those tools when I make the time, spend the energy, and get to work.

The perspectives and tools in this book don't have their own magic. They are tested and refined and represent the best of what we currently have to offer. But they can't do it alone.

You have an unprecedented opportunity to help usher in a new era of Compassionate Accountability that will give you, your employees, your team, and your organization a third way to transform the interactions that shape culture.

These tools, in your hands, can make a real difference. The next step is up to you.

PART I

THE BIG IDEA

Compassionate Accountability

CHAPTER 1

THE EVOLUTION
OF COMPASSION

I'VE BEEN exploring, studying, and teaching compassion my whole life. As a child, I lost track of how many times my parents admonished me by saying, "How would you feel if someone did that to you?" As I got a little older, the message changed to "Show some compassion" or "Walk a mile in their shoes." I learned that compassion meant showing empathy and practicing the Golden Rule.

I grew up as a Mennonite missionary kid in Africa. My father was a farmer from Kansas who got an advanced degree in animal husbandry and sought to solve the problem of protein deficiency among Congolese tribes in tropical climates. My mother was a nurse, helping solve the problems of malnutrition, disease, and poor hygiene. I learned that compassion meant alleviating suffering.

During my high school years in southern Africa in the 1980s, I saw firsthand the injustice and violence of racism and apartheid. Nelson Mandela, who held a vision of reuniting South Africa under a truly representative democracy, was in prison on Robben Island. I remember struggling with the pacifist teachings of my Mennonite faith. How could I respond to violence with kindness when everything is unjust and evil? When I turned eighteen I was required to register for the draft since I was a US citizen, even though I lived in Botswana. I registered as a conscientious objector, doing my best to articulate my support for my country but resistance to participating in war. I was taught that compassion meant avoiding violence and turning the other cheek.

I returned to America in 1985 to attend Bethel College, a small Mennonite liberal arts college in central Kansas. This experience opened my mind to different perspectives, engaged my critical thinking, and invited me to challenge my own beliefs. In this environment I learned that compassion meant being open-minded and tolerant of diversity.

My graduate training in clinical psychology at the University of Kansas during the early 1990s included a mediation certificate. When I was practicing mediation with a feuding couple, success meant finding a solution that both parties could live with and avoiding going to court. I learned that compassion meant finding a workable compromise.

As a clinical psychologist trained in the late 1990s, I was taught to show unconditional acceptance; be a "safe, nonanxious presence"; and attend to my client's feelings. Compassion in the therapy space meant helping clients feel safe, cared for, and valuable as human beings.

In the early 2000s I helped start an integrated behavioral medicine clinic at a regional hospital and discovered two more sides to compassion. As a liaison consultant within the healthcare environment, compassion meant coordinating care across diverse disciplines to keep the whole person at the center of it all.

At the same time, the mindfulness and meditation movement was hitting prime time, pioneered by the work of Jon Kabat-Zinn at the University of Massachusetts Medical School. I studied many of these emerging techniques and applied them in my treatment with patients who struggled with chronic, relapsing medical conditions. This movement has continued to evolve and grow. Now you can choose from dozens of smartphone apps that guide daily meditations and self-compassion exercises. In this context, compassion meant non-judgmental self-acceptance, presence, and self-care.

In 2008 I left clinical practice to start a professional leadership development company, motivated by the desire to make a bigger difference in a different context. I had been managing a multistate employee assistance program and noticed the prevalence of mental health problems in the workplace. I knew that most of the affected employees would never get professional mental health support but still needed the kind of help they weren't getting anywhere else. I also noticed how toxic many workplaces were. Employees didn't feel valued, leaders were overworked and caught between too much responsibility and too little authority, and corporate profit seeking was increasing income disparity. The 2008 recession only compounded these dynamics. Compassion in this context seemed pretty basic: treat your employees with fairness and dignity.

I feel so fortunate that the behavioral health organization in which I worked had an adventure ropes course. I seized the opportunity to get trained as an adventure course facilitator and started facilitating team building with corporate teams, students, and other community groups. Using an experiential process with teams to build cohesion, trust, and problem-solving skills was so rewarding. I saw potential for transformation within leaders, teams, and cultures and wanted to be part of that on a larger scale. I was fortunate to be trained and mentored by some of the greats in the adventure industry: Karl Rohnke, Tom Leahy, Michelle Cummings, Michael Gass, and the Project Adventure organization.

On the adventure course was the first place I began to experience the accountability aspect of compassion. On a high ropes course or even during an experiential learning activity on the ground, people need a balance of supportive acceptance and attention to boundaries and principles. A person's safety often depends on it. In this context, I experienced the tension between psychological safety and accountability for self-care. Whether doing a trust fall or helping your teammate scale a twelve-foot wall, each person must take 100 percent responsibility for their behaviors and roles while adhering to critical physical safety guidelines. At the same time, if people don't take absolute care of the psychological safety and acceptance of another's experience, participants can end up in risky situations or emotionally traumatized by the experience.

As an aside, the experiences that my partners and I shared on adventure courses at a previous employer before starting Next Element are part of what inspired the name of our company. A typical adventure course contains a variety of elements, each one designed to enable specific, positive growth experiences. A group will move from element to element depending on its goals for the experience. Facilitators often asked the group, "Are you ready to go to the next element?" We used to have a secret challenge among ourselves to see who could work in the phrase *next element* most often during the day without any clients knowing it.

Early on in my career as a clinical psychologist, I experienced the push for results. I was responsible for meeting quality and performance goals, completing documentation on time, and keeping my credentials current. As I began taking on leadership roles, I took on the added responsibility of holding others accountable for these same results. In these positions, I first began to appreciate that building connections and getting results go hand in hand. Compassion and accountability are not opposites; they should not compete with each other. Viewing them as such can take a leader down an unproductive path.

Since founding Next Element in 2008, we've gone all in on compassion. Our mission is to bring more compassion to the world. We've continued to study and explore what it means to be compassionate and how to make compassion accessible to more people. Over the years, we've seen a distinct progression in the way compassion is viewed and practiced in the workplace. We have struggled within our own company to reconcile connection and results.

Compassion's Journey

Compassion has been on an interesting journey over the last decade. I've segmented this journey into five eras: self-compassion, business compassion, inclusion compassion, pandemic compassion, and compassionate accountability. The date ranges are not absolute, and plenty of overlap exists between the eras. The main point is to capture how our relationship with compassion at work and in leadership has changed over time. See if you can relate to these shifts. Where were you in your journey as a leader during these eras? How did you experience these dynamics? Did you experience tension between connection and results?

Self-Compassion (before 2008)

Prior to the mid-2000s, compassion was seen as a personal practice, something that individuals could use to reduce stress, be more healthy, and expand their consciousness. Historical figures such as Mother Teresa, Gandhi, and the Dalai Lama were lifted up as models of compassion. Some workplaces recognized the importance of self-compassion, and some even supported their employees to pursue personal compassion practices under the banner of stress management or general wellness. But for the most part, compassion was a personal practice, or reserved for our heroes, not an integral part of corporate culture. Thankfully, research continues to show the benefits of compassion on wellness, and views have changed.

Business Compassion (2008 to Present)

A 2008 study on workplace conflict conducted by CCP Inc. found that US companies spent more than 2.8 hours per week dealing with conflict, which equated to approximately $359 billion in paid hours in 2008. In many cases, this severely crippled productivity and morale.[1] At the height of the Great Resignation during the COVID-19 pandemic, newer research reported in the *MIT Sloan Management Review* showed that toxic workplace culture is over ten times more important in driving people to leave their jobs than compensation.[2] Toxic cultures are rife with negative conflict where employees don't feel safe, empowered, or motivated. One of the biggest complaints of employees working in toxic work environments is that productivity and profit always get top priority at the expense of people and relationships.

Compassionate capitalism, as described in Blaine Bartlett's 2016 book, is a reaction to this trend. Bartlett blames uncontrolled, free-market capitalism for the rise of toxic work cultures. Results have become the only goal, and consequently, connection to others and the world in which we live has been lost. This has led to accountability without compassion. As an alternative, he promotes a model driven by enlightened self-interest, which balances business success with human and environmental consciousness.[3] He argues that enlightened self-interest actually produces better, more sustainable business outcomes while strengthening relationships between people and between humans and their environment—thus, accountability with compassion.

As data has accumulated on the negative impact of toxic work cultures on engagement, retention, productivity, and profitability, attention has turned toward how to humanize the workplace for better business results. *Awakening Compassion at Work*, by Jane Dutton and Monica Worline and published in 2017, offers a great synopsis of the research showing that strong relationships and respect for individuals can drive positive business results.[4] In 2020 the *Harvard Business*

Review published a summary of the literature showing that compassion in leadership improves collaboration, raises levels of trust, and enhances loyalty.[5] One promising healthcare-focused study showed that relational leadership practices, which include more compassion within the leadership culture, can have a stronger and more sustainable positive impact than tactical interventions, such as increased pay or flexible work schedules.[6]

Companies such as Google and LinkedIn led the early charge in creating more human-centered work environments. Google's research on team effectiveness showed that psychological safety was a key ingredient in high-performing teams.[7] LinkedIn was one of the pioneers in the movement to make compassion a central part of the workplace experience. Jeff Weiner was the CEO of LinkedIn from 2009 to 2020. He is regarded as one of the pioneers of compassionate workplaces for his systematic efforts to embed it into the culture. In 2018 Jeff appointed Scott Shute as head of Mindfulness and Compassion Programs, signaling a serious commitment to the philosophy that compassion is not only the right thing to do but also good for business. Scott's book, *The Full Body Yes*, articulates some of the principles he helped develop and teach at LinkedIn.[8]

The business compassion era helped us realize that a lack of compassion hurts business, while more compassion can help businesses realize even greater success without the negative consequences.

Inclusion Compassion (2017 to Present)

Diversity, equity, and inclusion (DEI) initiatives encourage self-awareness, cultural competency, and empathy in employees, addressing unconscious bias as well as promoting an overall safe, welcoming workplace environment. Diversity initiatives have been growing since long before 2017, but in the last several years, a focus on equity and inclusion has become a mainstream movement in corporate culture.

Gloria Cotton, one of the most respected voices for inclusion, defines inclusion this way: "Being a pro-inclusionist means creating specific actions to help every person feel welcomed, valued, respected, heard, understood and supported."[9]

Inclusion compassion is about recognizing the inherent value and contribution of all human beings and then taking steps to make this a reality in the workplace. Although organizations are implementing DEI within a range of levels, it's nearly impossible to be considered a leading employer without a well-developed DEI program, including appointing a top executive-level inclusion officer. *Fortune* is one of the most prominent publications that has added a ranking for companies based on their DEI efforts. This era positioned compassion as a foundation for inclusion.

Pandemic Compassion (2020 to 2021)

On January 9, 2020, the World Health Organization (WHO) announced a mysterious coronavirus-related pneumonia, first found in Wuhan, China. The first confirmed case in the United States was on January 21, 2020. On January 31, WHO announced a world health emergency. On February 3, the United States declared a public health emergency, and by March 11, WHO had officially announced COVID-19 as a pandemic.

Crisis can bring people together. Despite the political rhetoric, the one thing we all had in common was that we were afraid. "We are in this together" became the anthem. Somehow, when people are going through something difficult, just knowing we aren't alone can help tremendously. For a short time, the pandemic brought the world together in spirit.

The word *compassion* originates from the Latin root meaning "to suffer or struggle with." Worrying that the pandemic was probably going to get worse before it got better, and without a solution in sight, all we had was our shared suffering. Those were the good old days. Compassion took a big swing as the pandemic continued.

First, imagine a pendulum of compassion as shown in figure 1.1. A swing to the left represents more compassion. A swing to the right represents less compassion. We could apply this lens to any situation by asking ourselves, "What would it look like to respond with more compassion? Less compassion?"

March through June 2020 were the good old days for compassion. "We're all in this together" was the anthem. This represents a moderate level of compassion since it recognizes that others are also suffering and that we have something in common, something that unites us.

But how fast we can change and swing to the other extreme. Consider cancel culture: it has become common, almost normal, to viciously attack someone, attempt to destroy their reputation, or even resort to physical violence simply because we don't agree with their position or like their perspective on something. My belief is that cancel culture was made possible by the combination of ubiquitous and powerful social media, coupled with high-profile and influential leaders who modeled a willingness to use it as a weapon to further their own selfish agendas. This twisted attempt at accountability harbors no compassion.

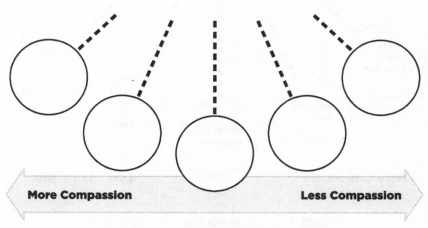

FIGURE 1.1. The pendulum of compassion.
Designed by Scott Light, CG Studios.

Let's take a look at how the pendulum swung during the first two years of the pandemic in figure 1.2.

I witnessed this firsthand a couple of years ago in my hometown. A local educator was accused of sexually assaulting a student. The investigation did not result in any formal charges, so some members of the community took matters into their own hands, launching a public cancel campaign against this person. The polarization caused by the publicity made it nearly impossible to engage in meaningful dialogue or pursue any form of restorative justice. This is an example of accountability without compassion.

Applying this to the pandemic, we saw extreme hatred and attacks between ideological groups formed around their beliefs about the virus, the cause, the vaccine, or how different groups should be treated. The vaxxer versus anti-vaxxer war ensued for nearly two years, with each side continually trying to discredit and vilify the other. Research showed significant differences along political party lines regarding vaccination status and beliefs about the virus. This certainly is evidence of less compassion since it focuses on differences rather than commonalities. How

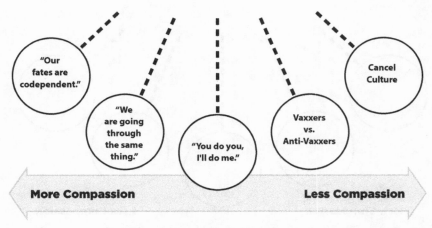

FIGURE 1.2. The pendulum of compassion during the COVID-19 pandemic. Designed by Scott Light, CG Studios.

quickly we went from "We are all in this together" to "You are a threat to our democracy since you don't agree with my position on COVID-19."

And then we have that in-between place, where compassion is neither noticeably present nor absent. The pendulum is at dead center.

I was a member of my church's elder leadership team from 2019 to 2021. During that time we agonized around the same issues every organization faced: How can we continue our mission and stay operational during the pandemic?

In fall 2021 we lifted the mask requirement in our church, leaving it open to personal choice. The next Sunday I showed up for church still wearing my mask. Among a couple dozen people who showed up that Sunday, I was one of only two who were wearing a mask. I was worried about being judged because I was in the minority. But it didn't happen. I didn't sense any negative energy in my interactions. I also didn't get any support. Nothing was said one way or the other.

The problem with the in-between place is that we basically allow people to do their thing, with an unspoken agreement not to say anything: "You do you, I'll do me" or "Let's agree to disagree." It's a no-man's-land where people coexist but without the intimacy and connection that comes when we embrace our interdependency and engage in healthy conflict.

The Solution: Compassionate Accountability

Compassion is so much more than most of us imagine or have experienced. I consider myself fortunate to have learned and experienced so many aspects of compassion—though even that learning was incomplete.

Compassion isn't just tolerance, safety, caring, empathy, alleviation of suffering, kindness, nonviolence, or even inclusion. Compassion means truly embracing that our fates are codependent. We aren't just going through the same trials, we truly are *in this together*. My actions affect you. Your actions affect me. My thoughts, beliefs, and feelings have a powerful impact on the world around me, and so do yours. Our world is inextricably connected. We get the biggest and best results through our connections, not in spite of them.

Compassion is what makes us human, keeps us on track, and brings us back together when we've lost our way.

Just being nice doesn't cut it. Compassion without accountability doesn't address the tough issues we are facing, nor does it acknowledge the inherent conflict when attempting to bring diverse viewpoints and skill sets together to solve big problems. Similarly, accountability without compassion results in toxic cultures that focus only on the end-game at the expense of people and relationships.

The next evolution of compassion is Compassionate Accountability.

Tom Henry, former learning and development coordinator at Whole Foods Market, has been heavily involved in the conscious capitalism movement. During an interview for my podcast, Tom shared with me one of the primary tenets of conscious capitalism, conscious culture, which implies and affirms, "We are in this together."[10] He went on to explain, "We are not separate individuals, we are a collective consciousness. Our fate as human beings is interdependent, so how we view and treat each other is critical to our survival and our ability to thrive." This idea is consistent with Charles Darwin's discovery that species who work together and depend on one another during tough times are more likely to survive and thrive.

Darwin's discovery applies even to the biggest organizations. During the COVID-19 pandemic, the WD-40 Company thrived and grew stronger thanks to its culture of compassion characterized by a safe and strong team-focused environment, transparent communication, consistent high standards, and leaders who modeled the company's values. WD-40 already had a long track record of success, but when many global organizations were struggling to survive and keep great talent, engagement at WD-40 went up to an all-time high. In 2021 98 percent of employees said they were excited to work there.

Garry Ridge, chairman and CEO of WD-40 for twenty-five years and up through the pandemic, credits its success to the company's compassionate culture, based on Garry's philosophy that a tribe is more successful than a team. Garry explained to me, "A team is something you play on. A tribe is something you belong to, like a family. Tribes feed and protect each other. Teams come and go, but tribes thrive over the long term." In his latest book, *The Unexpected Learning Moment: Lessons in Leading a Thriving Culture through Lockdown 2020*, Garry shares more specifics about how compassionate cultures can help organizations thrive during crisis.[11]

Dr. Rob McKenna, founder of WilD Leaders, is an industrial and organizational psychologist and leadership expert focusing on leading under pressure, with clients including Boeing, Microsoft, Heineken, and United Way. In my conversations with Rob, he has shared his deep conviction that we are in an unprecedented time in which whole and intentional leadership development matters.[12] We need leaders who can balance peacekeeping with truth speaking, lead with a sense of purpose, and see capability and potential instead of barriers.

Now more than ever, we need to bring compassion and accountability together, embracing both in full measure. Without it, the pendulum will keep swinging or, even worse, get stuck. If we want a better future and better companies, we need to invite people to prepare for this.

CHAPTER 2

COMPASSION AND ACCOUNTABILITY ARE COMPLEMENTARY

IN ALL THE YEARS I've worked with leaders, one of the most common questions I get asked is "How do you balance kindness, care, and concern with attention to results?" This noble question certainly gives voice to the struggle many leaders experience. The dilemma is expressed in many ways:

- You can't be someone's friend and boss at the same time.
- If you show vulnerability, people will take advantage of you.
- Sometimes you just have to bring the hammer down to show them who's boss.
- I've done everything I know to support them, and they still don't meet performance expectations.
- I don't want to be a jerk, but we need to get stuff done.
- I'd rather be respected than liked.
- We say we are human-centered, but we actually have a command-and-control culture.

- Being kind is great, but sometimes you have to be the bad cop.
- I'm just telling it like it is. That's honesty.
- We can't bring up conflicts in this team until we trust each other more.
- Sometimes you have to make people suffer to learn a lesson.
- I'm just practicing tough love.

Can you relate to any of these leadership philosophies and challenges? Do you tend toward being nice or holding people accountable? What's your default when situations become heated?

Leading industrial organizational psychologist Dr. Rob McKenna, who spent years studying leaders under pressure, found that people tend to slip to one extreme or the other in crucial moments. In his book *Composed: The Heart and Science of Leading under Pressure*, he describes peacekeepers as those who tend toward the compassion end of the spectrum, often compromising to keep the peace in the spirit of being nice. Truth speakers, on the other hand, tend toward the accountability end, defaulting to direct confrontation, telling it like it is.[1]

Whether you choose compassion or accountability, both paths include predictable compromises and negative consequences.

The Difference between Accountability and Responsibility

Throughout this book, you'll see the words *accountability* and *responsibility* being used a lot. Before we go any further, let's clarify the difference between these concepts as they relate to leadership.

Accountability and responsibility are big, heavy words, especially in leadership. I hear these words thrown around frequently in our work with leaders who are building more compassionate cultures. We've discovered that people misunderstand the difference between accountability and responsibility. Each concept is unique, and when leaders confuse the two, it can lead to frustration, trust problems, difficulty with execution, and potential burnout.

A leader is accountable to their organization for their own behaviors that help others deliver the results.

Leaders Are Accountable to Others

Accountability is when people have to answer to someone else about an outcome, metric, or end state. Usually this includes the key performance indicators of the arena they lead. If they are the CFO, they account for the financial performance of the organization. If they lead quality control, they are accountable for the quality metrics of the organization. If they are the manager of customer service, they must answer to the rest of the organization for the customer satisfaction ratings.

Leaders Are Responsible for Their Behaviors (No More, No Less)

The only thing a leader is responsible for is their own behavior. That's because we can control only our own behavior, not that of others. Obviously we try to influence the behavior of others, but we can't control it. We are not responsible for other people's behaviors.

Let me explain. Although leaders are accountable to others, they usually aren't the ones actually creating those outcomes.

As a CFO, I am accountable to my executive team regarding the financial performance of the organization, but I am not the one making daily spending decisions, giving raises, or generating leads for new business. All these behaviors contribute to the outcomes for which I am accountable, but they aren't my behaviors.

As the chief experience officer, I am accountable to my organization around our quality metrics. But I can't control and am not responsible for the choice that a customer service agent makes in the moment with an upset client.

The Consequences of Confusing
Accountability and Responsibility

When we confuse accountability and responsibility, we can easily get frustrated and overwhelmed. Have you ever heard a leader say, "The buck stops with me"? What does this mean? Many leaders take it to mean "Ultimately, I am responsible for things getting done." But this phrase has the opposite meaning: "Don't pass the buck on your responsibilities." As a leader, you should take responsibility for your own behaviors and let others do the same. If you try to take over or control one of your employee's behaviors, you have crossed the line and enabled them to pass the buck to you. That's because they are accountable *to* you, *for* their behavior.

I understand why a leader would be tempted to take over other people's behaviors. We feel a lot of pressure to perform. Our constituents, peers, and bosses are asking for results. They want to see the numbers trending in the right direction. Under pressure, a leader may try to take over responsibility for other people's behaviors in an attempt to meet expectations. But this isn't leadership. Sometimes when leaders get upset that people aren't doing their job or try to micromanage their people, I want to grab them by the shoulders and tell them, "Do your job. Be a leader."

What It Means to Hold People Accountable

Holding someone accountable means upholding a contract between people that goes something like this: "As the leader, I am accountable to my organization for the outcome of your performance. We have agreed on the following behaviors that contribute to our target outcomes. You are accountable to me and your team for these behaviors. My job is not to do your job but to help you execute those behaviors consistently and effectively."

Being accountable to others around outcomes that someone else is delivering requires a unique understanding of roles, boundaries, and responsibilities.

The whole notion of holding someone accountable implies that the other person is responsible for the behavior, but I care or am connected enough to the outcome to make sure it gets done.

How Leaders Hold People Accountable

A leader is not responsible for the behavior of their employees. But they are ultimately accountable to their organization for the results.

Here is a list of leadership-specific behaviors over which leaders have control and are uniquely responsible for executing:

- Clarifying and communicating vision, expectations, and goals
- Giving frequent and clear feedback about progress and performance
- Teaching, mentoring, and building capability in others but not doing it for them
- Helping people maintain focus on what they are responsible for, not what they can't control
- Helping employees see the connection between their behaviors and the organization's purpose
- Offering affirmation, recognition, support, and other methods to enhance employee engagement and motivation
- Executing consequences within their scope of authority, such as firing, promotion, discipline, or incentives

You've probably seen the consequences when leaders confuse accountability and responsibility. The results are lowered morale, confusion of roles, poor execution, and ultimately a leader who is tired, stressed out, unsatisfied, and ineffective.

Let's review what can happen when leaders fall victim to the false dichotomy of compassion versus accountability. Here are typical behaviors, compromises, and consequences of leaders who practice compassion without accountability:

- Believe empathy and support are sufficient motivators of behavior
- Avoid difficult conversations and conflict
- View accountability as uncaring and mean
- Compromise their own boundaries to avoid conflict
- Delay or fail to execute proper consequences
- Use common mottos such as "Be nice," "Don't hurt other people's feelings," "Put yourself in her shoes," "Don't raise your voice"
- Often help others in ways that create dependence and invite resentment
- Regularly jump in to clean up messes, put out fires, or finish projects
- Obtain consensus but not commitment
- Have a team with poor follow-through and low confidence
- Experience the same problems, which never get solved
- Are liked but not respected
- Struggle with problems of engagement, retention, and morale

Here are typical behaviors, compromises, and consequences of leaders who practice accountability without compassion:

- Believe rules, consequences, and expectations are sufficient motivators of behavior
- Are quick to confront and question others' motives
- Use threats, ultimatums, or passive-aggressive tactics, especially during conflict

- Have all the answers and avoid listening
- Disregard other people's boundaries to get things done
- View compassion as a sign of weakness
- Use common mottos such as "Failure is not an option," "We need to teach people to respect authority," "Don't show weakness," "Do it because I said so"
- Obtain compliance, but not engagement or loyalty
- Have team members with low morale and trust who tend to compete with each other
- Are feared but not respected
- Struggle with problems of engagement, retention, and morale

Neither option is a leadership success strategy. *Compassion without accountability gets you nowhere. Accountability without compassion gets you alienated.* Flip-flopping between the two doesn't work either, so how do we reconcile these seemingly contradictory approaches to leadership?

Balance Is the Wrong Question

The problem with the question of balance is that it's the wrong question. Behind this question and all the examples above is the assumption that compassion and accountability are opposites, that you can have one or the other but not both—or at least not at the same time.

From my experience, I've seen that most of what trips leaders up and creates negative cultures is their mindset that compassion and accountability are in opposition. If I believe that kindness and caring will solve all problems, then accountability is certainly out of the question. Similarly, if I am a strong proponent of accountability, it's easy to believe that compassion isn't for me or at least represents a weak compromise.

The truth is that compassion and accountability are not in tension and don't need to be balanced. Real compassion includes and requires accountability. In fact, compassion without accountability isn't even compassion. And accountability without compassion is simply inhumane. They can't exist alone and were never meant to. Leaders don't have to choose, and they don't have to perform a balancing act. Embracing both in full measure is the key to transformation and breakthrough.

Compassion Is about Struggling *With*

As I noted earlier, the word *compassion* originates from the Latin root meaning "to suffer or struggle with." Stated another way, compassion is about struggling alongside another person. It doesn't necessarily mean "to take away the suffering." This misconception can often create a barrier to effective leadership.

Imagine if you viewed compassion as a process of struggling with others toward better solutions rather than trying to take away the struggle. I firmly believe that the purpose of life isn't to get rid of the struggle but instead to find the meaning in the struggle.

This mindset about the goal of compassion is fundamentally different. Viewing compassion as a process of suffering or struggling with others can make a huge difference in how leaders approach their own and others' challenges because it emphasizes interdependence.

What Is Compassionate Accountability?

Compassionate Accountability is the process of building connection while also getting results. What does this look like in action? Douglas Conant knows firsthand because he used these accountability skills to turn around a troubled company. Doug, now founder and CEO of ConantLeadership, is also an internationally renowned Fortune 500 business leader, bestselling author, and the leader who turned around a struggling Campbell Soup Company during his tenure as CEO (2001–2011). He came into a challenging situation in which the culture had deteriorated, people weren't being held accountable, and the company was lagging behind its competition. Many "turnaround CEOs" would come in with guns blazing, clean house, and then move on to the next gig. And while Doug did have to replace 300 of the top 350 leaders in his first eighteen months as CEO, he also had a bold vision for engaging every remaining stakeholder and earning trust, which was to *"Help build high-trust, high-performance teams that honor people, defy the critics, and thrive in the face of adversity."*[2]

That sounds like a tall order. How did he accomplish this at Campbell Soup? By practicing his philosophy: *"Be tough-minded on standards and tenderhearted with people."*[3]

Doug told me that this philosophy has to be evident in every single interaction.[4] He believes that "the action is in the interaction." Doug estimates that leaders have between two hundred and four hundred interactions per day of less than two minutes and that a leader's legacy will be dependent on how they handle those interactions. In his book *TouchPoints: Creating Powerful Leadership Connections in the Smallest of Moments*, he outlines how leaders can build the kinds of compassion connections that bring people together and also deal with the difficult issues.[5] "A leader's legacy will be dependent on how they handle those interactions."

You Don't Have to Choose or Compromise

Several years ago, we were engaged by a national service company to build Compassionate Accountability with their 250 regional call-center managers. These managers all worked remotely, supporting and supervising a national network of agents doing the daily work of serving customers. This was part of a corporate initiative to make work more enjoyable and satisfying.

The most consistent complaint among these call-center managers was that they felt drained by their interactions with the agents they supervised. The managers were accountable to the organization for specific performance goals among their agents, but they struggled to meet standards. Frequent conversations led to temporary improvements, but many agents didn't sustain the changes. Managers believed they were doing all they could to support their agents, offering solutions and second chances and hoping things would get better. Many dreaded the conversations around performance metrics. One manager described her daily performance check-in calls with agents as "picking scabs." The organization as a whole was not meeting its performance objectives, managers didn't know what else to do, and they weren't enjoying their daily interactions.

We engaged these managers to practice Compassionate Accountability by paying equal attention to three fundamental components in every interaction: value, capability, and responsibility. We asked them to evaluate their behavior according to these three criteria:

- What behaviors affirm and uphold your *value* as a human? What behaviors affirm and uphold the *value* of your agents?
- What behaviors affirm and uphold your *capability* as a manager? What behaviors affirm and uphold the *capability* of your agents?
- What behaviors affirm and uphold your *responsibility* as a manager? What behaviors affirm and uphold the *responsibility* of your agents?

Here's what they discovered. They were able to answer the questions about value, although their answers were a bit one-sided. They were kind, caring, and considerate and had a ton of empathy for the agents. Many of these managers had been promoted from agents and certainly understood their struggle. But the managers weren't affirming and upholding their own value. They were frequently drained after conversations. They were frustrated that agents didn't sustain performance goals. They didn't enjoy their work. Some were losing enthusiasm and wondered what they were doing wrong. This wasn't sustainable. Correcting this problem required them to affirm and uphold their own value by acknowledging their own emotions and experiences and asking for help.

Regarding the second questions about capability, these managers tended to fall on the opposite extreme. They treated themselves as much more capable than their agents. Rather than engaging the agents in finding sustainable solutions to the performance problems, they kept coming with more advice, ideas, and solutions based on their own experiences. They thought they were helping, but all they were doing was creating passive dependence and inviting resentment. Their behavior inadvertently reinforced the idea that the agents weren't capable of solving their own problems. In social psychology terms, we call this *learned helplessness*.

Correcting this problem meant actually doing less. Managers needed to hold back, listen more, invite their agents to step up, and give space for them to think for themselves. Managers struggled with this because they had become conditioned to think a leader's job is to have answers and solve problems. In fact, they were probably promoted for that very reason—most leaders are, which is where the Peter principle comes from.[6]

Named after Laurence J. Peter, a management researcher in the 1960s, the Peter principle describes a phenomenon where employees are promoted based on their success in previous jobs until they reach a level at which they are no longer competent since current job skills don't necessarily translate into new job skills.

We promote leaders to their level of incompetence. In most cases, the higher up a leader is promoted, the more their success depends on social and emotional skills such as compassion, communication, and conflict negotiation. However, they are promoted for their technical competencies and knowledge of the job rather than their ability to lead people. This promotion sets them up for failure, and many leaders aren't aware, aren't prepared, and don't receive the training and support to make that transition. How many of your leadership job descriptions have these competencies spelled out?

The third pair of questions revealed the biggest gap in these leaders' practice of Compassionate Accountability. They acknowledged that while they had clear standards of performance, they weren't affirming and upholding their responsibilities or the responsibilities of their agents. They weren't having candid and direct conversations with them about their goals, nor were they talking about consequences for not meeting those objectives. By avoiding tough conversations, they were sending the message "We are tenderhearted with people and don't actually care about standards." No wonder agents didn't sustain the changes. They didn't have to. They didn't appreciate how these goals connected with the company's mission or see that their managers cared about it. They came to expect empathy, get spoon-fed another solution, and be given a second, third, or fourth chance to fix the problem.

When confronted with this realization, many of the managers took a step back. They gave all the possible excuses, but they couldn't deny the reality. Their behavior was not really compassionate. They were sacrificing their well-being, undermining their agents' growth and development, compromising corporate standards and goals, and ultimately not meeting performance metrics—all under the illusion of being nice.

The biggest fear many managers had was that if they began to affirm and uphold responsibility, they would alienate their agents and damage the relationship. They also feared the inevitable conflict involved in having necessary but difficult conversations.

The first thing these managers needed was hope that they wouldn't be forced to choose compassion or accountability. We explained to them that the tension they were feeling wasn't between compassion and accountability. The tension was between compassion and drama. All the behaviors that were holding them back were neither compassionate nor accountable. They were all drama-based behaviors.

Drama is what happens when we respond to conflict by struggling against ourselves or each other, with or without awareness, to feel justified about our unhealthy behaviors. When it comes to drama, we set up win-or-lose situations. That's not compassion. Most drama is habitual while compassion is intentional. With drama we seek justification rather than what's best for all. Drama is self-serving while compassion pays equal attention to self, others, and the greater good.

With an option for a new path forward, we reassured them that they didn't have to compromise. If they committed to valuing themselves equally and disclosed to the agents their pain, this vulnerability would build a stronger connection and reinforce shared struggle.

We assured them that if they stepped back from trying to solve their agents' problems, this might be tough at first, but over time the agents would appreciate being trusted and encouraged to solve their own problems. Feeling capable is much better than feeling dependent and resentful. We shared an old saying made popular by Ken Blanchard, "Those who plan the battle rarely battle the plan."[7] Although it was tough to accept, these managers truly wished deep down for their agents to be successful. All they had to do was let go of their ego's need to be the savior.

Finally we reminded these leaders that responsibility doesn't exist in a vacuum. Inviting higher levels of responsibility can occur only when we are also tending to value and capability.

To correct the responsibility gap, leaders began to talk explicitly about standards, review the numbers, and discuss consequences for failing to meet the standards.

Putting it all together, their new conversations went something like this. See if you can notice where they made corrections on the way they affirmed and upheld their own and others' value, capability, and responsibility.

I'm struggling with something, and I want your help. I've been feeling drained from our interactions and don't feel effective as a manager. I realize that I've been working so hard to support you and solve your problems that I haven't allowed or expected you to be part of the solution. I'm interested in your ideas about how you can consistently close the gap. I haven't done right by our organization either because I haven't held myself or you accountable to meet its goals. Meeting your performance goals is nonnegotiable, and we have standard consequences that I will begin to enforce. I care about you, and I want you to be successful.

In this scenario, I hope you can sense the shift in struggle. Instead of struggling *alone, against,* or *instead of,* these managers were redefining what it means to struggle *with.* They showed compassion and accountability without compromise or drama.

Four months after the training, we convened for a check-in meeting to report on progress, share stories, and answer questions. We also shared outcomes data that had been collected from the 250 managers.

In all our programs, we track changes in self-efficacy: a person's confidence in their ability to apply new behaviors to meet particular challenges. We measure changes in their confidence to be open, resourceful, and persistent, three critical components of Compassionate Accountability. Often we ask participants to assess their efficacy in multiple contexts so we can see the differential impact of the intervention at home, at work, or in their team.

Table 2.1 shows changes in self-efficacy associated with this program. Change is expressed in terms of effect size, which demonstrates the direction and magnitude of change.

An effect size measures the magnitude of change in a group of scores, expressed in terms of standard deviation units. In other words, how much did the average self-efficacy score improve? An effect size of .25 means that the average score increased by .25 standard deviations. This is considered educationally significant—in this instance, that

TABLE 2.1. Effect sizes for change in self-efficacy among regional call-center managers completing Compassionate Accountability training

	Openness	Resourcefulness	Persistence
Me at home	0.23	0.10	0.20
Me at work	0.44	0.12	0.31
My team	0.46	0.17	0.36

people learned something. Effect sizes of .50 are considered clinically significant, meaning a deeper level of transformation.

I want to highlight several important findings. First, notice the strong positive changes in openness within the context of "Me at work" and "My team." This reflects the corrective behavior of getting more vulnerable about their own struggles. Changes in resourcefulness were minimal, which was to be expected. We asked them to do less to solve agents' problems. Improvements in persistence reflected managers' corrective behaviors of being clear on standards and following through on consequences.

Managers were also asked to report on the impact of this training in various areas of their lives. This data is shown in table 2.2.

These changes are remarkable, especially considering that these managers were involved in a variety of other performance-improvement initiatives during that time. To measure incremental impact, we asked them to estimate the impact attributable to this program separately from other training initiatives. In all four areas, they reported over 50 percent improvement *over and above* everything else they were doing.

As much as I love hard data, the personal stories are the ones I save in my heart and the reason I go to work every day. Here are some of the comments we heard from managers:

TABLE 2.2. Percentage change in four areas of focus that regional call-center managers attribute to Compassionate Accountability training

Area of impact	Percent improvement attributed to Compassionate Accountability training
Personal relationships	54 percent
Work relationships	59 percent
Leadership skills	57 percent
Teamwork	56 percent

- "With a few surprisingly simple changes in my approach, a chronically underperforming manager has met or exceeded her performance metrics for four months in a row."
- "My employees used to dread our check-ins. Now we both experience them as 'We are in this together.' I have so much more positive energy."
- "An eye-opener when learning new ways to recircuit my brain to a better understanding of bringing a situation to a satisfactory conclusion on both sides."

If compassion without accountability gets you nowhere, and accountability without compassion gets you alienated, then what does Compassionate Accountability look like in practice? I invite you to turn to part 2 to learn about the compassion mindset.

Main Points

- If we view compassion and accountability as opposites, we place them in competition with each other and have no choice but to choose a side or try to balance them.

- Balance is the wrong question. *Compassion* means "to suffer or strug-gle with." Accountability is already embedded within compassion. Compassion requires accountability; they aren't separate.
- Leaders no longer have to choose compassion or accountability, be a flip flopper, or engage in a tenuous balancing act between them. You can have both without compromising either.
- Compassionate Accountability can infuse every interaction and requires us to simultaneously affirm and uphold that people are valuable, capable, and responsible.

PART II

THE MODEL

The Compassion Mindset

CHAPTER 3

WHAT IS THE COMPASSION MINDSET?

WORK RELATIONSHIPS should energize us, not drain us. Drama steals too much precious time and energy away from what's most important. Compassion is what makes us human, brings us together, and gets us back on track when we lose our way. Compassion is the antidote to drama.

Compassion matters. Compassion works.

We need more compassion in our world and workplaces. Every leader has an opportunity to make that happen.

Compassion must not come at the expense of accountability, though, because our missions and goals are too important to compromise. At the same time, our people are our greatest asset, so we must prioritize the human being at the center of it all. Thankfully, we don't have to choose.

With Compassionate Accountability, leaders can reimagine their understanding and practice of compassion to include accountability without giving up either one. No drama, no compromises.

Interactions, Cultures, and Brands

Bobby Herrera is the cofounder and chief executive officer of the human resources service company Populus Group. With an annual revenue of $500 million and many Fortune 500 customers, Populus Group is one of the fastest-growing companies in the United States. Bobby has discovered that brand is a lagging indicator of the quality of your culture. This means that you can pour all you want into fancy marketing, branding, and image management, but if your culture stinks, so will your brand.

The obvious next question is, What is culture? Culture can be defined in many ways, but I prefer simple and elegant ones. The most elegant I've heard comes from Seth Godin, who has a gift for cutting through the clutter: "People like us do things like this."

At its core, culture is the sum of every interaction between the people. This includes interactions between employees, between leaders, between leaders and followers, between employees and customers, and even between members of the organization and the general public.

Because of this, leaders have to be fluid in the small moments and offer an opportunity to practice compassion.

Previously I introduced you to Doug Conant, the CEO who turned around Campbell Soup with the philosophy of being tough-minded on standards and tenderhearted with people. He also recognized that life is too fragmented and dynamic to rely on traditional approaches to communication. Now more than ever, leaders need behavioral skills to make a difference in the smallest moments in the flow of work. Figure 3.1 shows how it plays out.

FIGURE 3.1. Interactions, culture, brand.
Designed by Scott Light, CG Studios.

Your brand is a lagging indicator of the quality of your culture. Culture is the sum of all the interactions between your people. The action is in the interaction. Embedding Compassionate Accountability within every interaction will create a thriving culture and lead to a strong brand.

How do we enable leaders to be fluid with compassion in the small moments but also provide a shared vision, mindset, and behavioral skill set that can be adopted across an organization? Let's start with a working definition of compassion that captures its full essence and purpose: *Compassion is the practice of demonstrating that people are valuable, capable, and responsible in every interaction.* This definition has four important parts:

- *Practice*—Compassion is a behavioral skill set. The more we work at it, the better we get. This reinforces that compassion is a learnable skill.
- *Demonstrating*—Compassion is more than a feeling, concept, or principle. It must be observable through behavior. Unless we can all agree on observable behaviors, we can't measure or teach it, set goals around it, or see if we are making progress.
- *Valuable, capable, and responsible*—These three aspects of compassion are all necessary but not sufficient on their own. They work together and rely on each other. This reinforces that compassion is not in competition with accountability.
- *In every interaction*—Every moment counts. Every conversation is an opportunity to be compassionate.

For compassion to become synonymous with your brand, it has to permeate the DNA of your culture. To be present throughout your culture, it has to show up in the daily interactions. To do this, it has to become a mindset.

What Is the Compassion Mindset?

Wayne Dyer, an author and motivational speaker, said, *"When you change the way you look at things, the things you look at change."*

In chapter 13, I explain our quest to discover why some people seem to fly when presented with an opportunity to learn and grow, while others seem to stay stuck on the ground. The short preview is we identified three kinds of people: lifelong learners, cautious skeptics, and saboteurs. All were smart, motivated, and talented. What distinguished these people from each other, however, was their mindset. The Lifelong Learners had a growth mindset that viewed themselves and others as valuable, capable, and responsible.

After recognizing this, we set out to create a model. At the time, we had lists and words and diagrams on the whiteboard in our office, but we were trying to find a simple and elegant visual. I credit my colleague Aaron Chappell Deckert for a breakthrough moment. At one point, he leaned back in his chair, closed his eyes for a while, and then reflected out loud, "I see switches, as if energy is flowing through them. When they are on, energy flows. When they are off, energy is blocked."

Brilliant! Being the action-oriented person that I am, I ran with it. We then had three switches, each representing one of the three components of compassion: value, capability, and responsibility. When the switches are on, energy flows. When they are off, energy is blocked. I ran to the local hardware store and purchased a three-switch outlet cover and three switches.

As we played with our new invention, we came upon another question. If a light switch is labeled as on or off, how does that metaphor translate into the dimensions of value, capability, and responsibility? This took a little more time as we evaluated the attitudes and behaviors that indicated each switch was on or off. What descriptor would best capture how people see themselves and others when their switches are on, off, or somewhere in between?

Figure 3.2 shows what we first came up with, my hardware store version, which I still use today in training programs. Figure 3.3 shows our spiffed up model.

We were so excited. We called in Jamie Remsberg, my cofounder I've been with on this journey since the beginning. We showed her our model and gave her a brief explanation, anticipating and hoping she'd be speechless with amazement. Jamie responded, "I get it! This describes what we've been doing and teaching since the beginning."

People say there's nothing new under the sun. But that doesn't mean we can't keep searching for more accessible and impactful ways to apply what we know. Better models and frameworks help us teach others faster and with greater impact.

Don't worry if you don't know what all the labels mean. We'll discuss them in the next chapter, as well as how to know whether your switches are on or off and how to apply this framework to all sorts of leadership challenges. For now, let's focus on the benefits of the model.

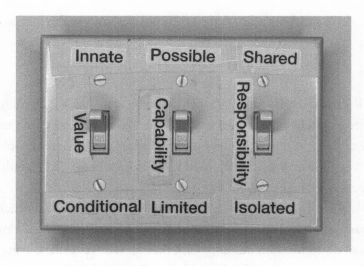

FIGURE 3.2. The original three switches.
Photo by Nate Regier.

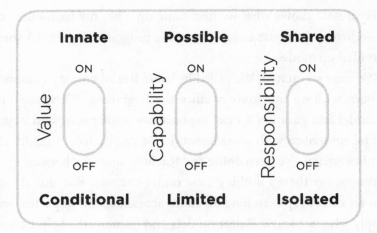

FIGURE 3.3. The official three switches of a compassion mindset.
Designed by Scott Light, CG Studios.

My litmus test for a good model is that it must meet these three criteria:

1.   You can draw it on a bar napkin and explain it in thirty seconds.
2.   Within two minutes, it can resonate with a person's pain.
3.   Within five minutes, it can give hope for a new path.

I'll let you be the judge of this when you start using and applying the three-switches model. Meanwhile, I'd like to share my first experience trying it out with leaders. Like a craftsman with a new tool, we started experimenting with our new model and seeing what it could do long before we had an operator's guide.

We were contacted by the HR director of a large construction company serving clients in several states across the Southwest United States to do some team building with their executive team. During my discovery process with the HR director, I learned that the company was family owned and that some tension had been building between the father and son regarding succession. Apparently, other members of the executive team were feeling the tension and often got caught in the crossfire. Feeling some trepidation and knowing that these types of situations can get messy and drawn out, I asked the HR director what success would look like in her view.

"Normally, father and son can't be in the same room for very long before one of them starts yelling obscenities and storms out. They have offices off the same hallway but haven't talked to each other for months. Success would be if they could get through one session without swearing and stomping out."

I don't enjoy negative conflict, but I decided we had little to lose, so we accepted the job. For the first session, I invited the executive team to gather at our office, a neutral location, hoping this would help create a safer place for dialogue. When everyone arrived, I was surprised how cordial they were. Father and son were professional and seemed to be on their best behavior.

Whenever we work with teams, we establish basic rules of engagement, which we call *behavior norms*. In chapter 7, I provide a template for how to develop your own behavior norms. Usually I share a few basic nonnegotiable rules and open it up to the group to codevelop a social contract. But this time I decided to use our new tool instead. I drew the three switches on the whiteboard, explained what they meant, and asked if the group could commit to keeping their switches on during our time together. Everyone agreed.

Things were going along just fine, and we were about an hour into our session when the father fired a shot across the bow. The son had commented about how he didn't feel included and wished the team would mentor and guide him to learn the ropes, especially if he was to take over the company. He looked directly at his father when he said "the team." The father popped off a sarcastic comment about how his son was too interested in his hobbies and couldn't understand the construction business anyway. The son stood up from his chair and started to gather his stuff, and I could see the blood rising in his face.

I jumped in and called a quick time-out, asking the son to sit down. He did so but was clearly on the verge of an explosion. I turned to the father and directed his attention to the three switches. "Just now, when you said that to your son, I'm curious, where were your switches?"

The father looked at the whiteboard, reflected for a few seconds, and replied, "My switch of capability was off. I didn't see my son as capable of taking over the company."

My next question was "Hypothetically, if your capability switch was on, how might you approach this situation with your son differently?"

Without skipping a beat, the father looked directly at his son and said, "I would take the time to teach you and mentor you. I know you are smart and capable."

Tears welled up in the son's eyes. His posture relaxed, and he sank back into his chair. The room was dead quiet. Judging from the expressions on the other executive's faces, they were shocked and had no idea what just happened.

I'd love to report that this moment changed everything for this leadership team and this father-son relationship. It didn't. The next hour was tense, but nobody dropped the f-bomb, and nobody stormed out. When the team left, the conversation was almost friendly. The HR director was ecstatic.

The significance of this moment wasn't that the father and son changed their behavior overnight. The significance was that mindset matters, and the idea of turning on the capability switch enabled the father to visualize, even for a brief moment, a different story. It even allowed him to role-play the behavior that could change their situation for the better.

Since then we've experienced over and over how the three switches of the compassion mindset can stick, resonate, and kindle hope by lighting up a different path. When our switches are on and we treat ourselves and others as valuable, capable, and responsible, energy flows in a positive direction to build connection, engagement, innovation, ownership, loyalty, and thriving cultures. When our switches are off, energy is blocked and wasted, which ends up causing division, disengagement, drama, and cultures that languish.

We hope that this model can do the same for you and anyone else who is searching for a path to more human-centered leadership without compromise.

Assess Your Compassion Mindset

In the next three chapters, you will gain insight and practical strategies for turning on and keeping on your three switches as a leader. And you will be able to apply this beyond yourself to explore how it works to transform culture. To get started, here's a quick survey to assess your mindset.

Table 3.1 lists six principles associated with the compassion mindset. For each one, first indicate how strongly you embrace that principle and second, how often you practice that principle with yourself and others.

There's no right or wrong score, but the higher you rate yourself, the more you embrace and embody the compassion mindset in your life. If you are using this book as part of a personal or professional development program, use your score as a baseline. Then, you can set goals for yourself and reevaluate later on.

TABLE 3.1. The compassion mindset survey

Compassion mindset principle	How strongly do you embrace this principle? 0 = not at all, 5 = completely	How often do you practice this principle with yourself and others? 0 = none of the time, 5 = all of the time
People are unconditionally valuable and deserve to be respected.	_____	_____
Even if someone makes a mistake or fails to perform, they are still worthwhile as a person.	_____	_____
People are capable of positive change and contribution.	_____	_____
Under the right conditions, anyone can contribute.	_____	_____
Pointing fingers gets us further away from a solution.	_____	_____
No matter what happened before, we share responsibility for what happens next.	_____	_____
Total score	_____ / 30	_____ / 30

Main Points

- With Compassionate Accountability, leaders can reimagine their understanding and practice of compassion to include accountability without giving up either one. No drama, no compromises.

- Brand is driven by culture, which is driven by daily interactions. Leaders must become fluid with compassion in the small moments if they want to change the interactions that drive culture and create strong brands.
- Compassion is the practice of demonstrating that people are valuable, capable, and responsible in every interaction.
- The compassion mindset is a decision and attitude that views the self and others as valuable, capable, and responsible.
- The three switches of the compassion mindset are value, capability, and responsibility. Each one can be assessed through observable behaviors. When they are turned on, people can experience more connection, engagement, innovation, ownership, and loyalty and a thriving culture.
- Survey your compassion mindset by identifying how strongly you embrace and embody the six fundamental principles.

CHAPTER 4

THE VALUE SWITCH

THE FIRST SWITCH of the compassion mindset is the switch of value. When the switch is on, we believe and behave in ways that affirm innate value. When the switch is off, we believe value is conditional and behave in ways that reinforce this belief, as shown in figure 4.1.

FIGURE 4.1. The value switch.
Designed by Scott Light, CG Studios.

Turning on the value switch involves the fundamental belief that people *are unconditionally valuable.*

What does this mean? Everyone deserves to be valued for who they are as a person, no strings attached. This applies especially to our unique experiences, perspectives, and emotions.

Before we go any further, let's take a quick quiz. Using this initial definition of what it means to have our value switch on, evaluate the interactions listed in table 4.1. The correct answers are at the end of this chapter in table 4.4, along with commentary to help with deeper understanding and application.

When the Value Switch Is Off

When the value switch is off, we view our own or another person's value as conditional, which means we allow conditions such as individual differences, group affiliations, past experience, or performance to influence our perception of a person's value.

These five clusters of observable behaviors let us know that the value switch is off:

- Minimizing feelings and experiences
- Hiding feelings and experiences
- Viewing personal feelings and experiences as a liability or weapon
- Attacking, judging, and excluding those who are different
- Avoiding vulnerability

Minimizing Feelings and Experiences

Our personal experiences and emotions are integral to who we are as people. Being human means we feel. Minimizing feelings is indicative of turning off our value switch. For ourselves, maybe we don't think anyone would care, or we've convinced ourselves that our feelings

TABLE 4.1. Value switch interactions quiz

What you observe	Is the value switch on? Y/N
1. Your gut tells you something's not right. You decide to speak up even though you are unsure how it will be received.	_____
2. You ask someone how they are coping with a difficult change at work, and they respond, "You gotta do what you gotta do."	_____
3. You ask your boss to help you deal with a coworker who seems to be sabotaging your efforts on the team. She responds by telling you, "He's just jealous."	_____
4. Someone confides in you about a challenge, and you tell them about a bigger challenge you had, reassuring them, "It could be worse."	_____
5. You appropriately confront an employee about a performance problem, and she responds by saying, "I don't feel safe right now."	_____
6. You confront the most assertive person in the meeting and ask them to stop interrupting so your more introverted peer can finish what she was saying.	_____
7. You share a concern with your boss about a coworker's behavior, and he responds, "Why are you getting so upset?"	_____
8. You are a white American male, and your coworker is a female from India. You tell her, "I feel awkward because I don't always know how I come across to you."	_____

aren't as important as those of others, so we stay quiet to keep the peace. For others, we might dismiss or devalue a person's feelings as if they aren't relevant or don't matter. When we do this, we send the message that they are less valuable as a human.

Hiding Feelings and Experiences

Hiding feelings is another symptom of our value switch being turned off. We all have our reasons for doing it. Maybe we've experienced others misusing or abusing our vulnerability in the past, or we've been taught that sharing our own feelings is weak and unprofessional. As a result, we've adopted the false belief that others can define our value by how they respond to us.

Regardless of our reasons, the behavioral result of hiding is that we keep our feelings out of view of others. By doing this, we deprive others of seeing us for who we are or of being able to support us. By hiding our feelings, we treat them as illegitimate, defective, or invisible while also devaluing ourselves in the process.

Viewing Personal Feelings and Experiences as a Liability or Weapon

Feelings can also be viewed as a liability or weapon. When we view feelings as weak, we imply that a person's value is dependent on removing feelings or at least keeping them under control. We also can use feelings as a weapon. Emotional hijacking occurs when someone uses feelings to divert attention away from the real issue or avoid accountability for their behavior.

Attacking, Judging, and Excluding Those Who Are Different

When we see value as conditional, we see divergence as a threat. Individual differences are viewed as a threat to the status quo, power and control structures, or our own identity. Whenever we view diversity as a threat, we send the message that showing who you truly are will get you hurt or alienated. As a result, we judge, attack, and exclude those who are different. Value is conditional on being the same and fitting in.

Avoiding Vulnerability

When our value switch is off, we feel vulnerable whenever we allow our emotions and personal experiences to come to the surface because we've made value conditional on being strong, being the same, and keeping our personal issues behind closed doors.

When the value switch is off, the result is an unsafe, toxic environment in which people are judged and excluded.

Turn On Your Value Switch

Because people are valuable, everyone deserves to be heard, affirmed, safe, invited, and included.

Dr. Rob McKenna, whose organization WiLD Leaders worked with hundreds of leaders throughout the COVID-19 pandemic, made this observation and conclusion: *"The pandemic gave us a front-row seat to the brokenness and capacity in people around the world. We need to invest in people in a way that is an invitation to their humanity."*[1]

How do we invite people into their humanity? How do we turn on the value switch? Here are nine behavioral strategies that any leader can begin practicing and any organization can integrate into its culture:

- Listen to and validate feelings without judging.
- Assume positive intentions, and check assumptions.
- Affirm experiences, even if you can't relate.
- Empathize by finding common emotional ground.
- Be transparent by sharing your own feelings, motives, and experiences.

- Embrace vulnerability.
- Remember that you don't have to agree with someone to value them as a person.
- Separate the person from the behavior.
- Include and leverage diversity.

Listen to and Validate Feelings without Judging

Listening to another person's feelings and experiences can be transformational. Tom Henry, a values-based leadership consultant, gets it. Professionally, he has extensive experience in retail, leadership, and executive development, having experienced tremendous change over the past thirty-five years, including the retail implosion of the 1980s and '90s, which led to the rise of the digital economy. Most recently he was the learning and development coordinator for Whole Foods Market. Tom grew up in Virginia during the 1950s and '60s, when Jim Crow laws were in force, and was in the first integrated high school class to graduate in 1971. He has attended historically white and historically Black colleges, weathered the turbulent times of Vietnam, Woodstock, the fight for gay rights, and the AIDS crisis.

Tom is heavily involved in the conscious capitalism movement. When I spoke with Tom, I asked him what compassion means for leaders.[2] For Tom, the most compassionate action we can take for another person is to listen to them. When we listen, we see them for who they are, without judgment or conditions. When we connect authentically at a deep level of listening, we also keep our own value switch on because we allow the possibility of transforming from our limited ego perspective.

The following are examples of what this looks like:

- "How are you doing?"
- "It's okay to tell me how you are doing."
- "How are you feeling?"
- "Your feelings matter to me."

- "I care about how you are feeling."
- "Your feelings are real and important."
- "I'm here to listen."
- "You are okay just the way you are."
- "How you are feeling is perfectly okay."

This attitude and these types of statements are particularly difficult for people who view their job as a technician. They approach situations through the lens of problem-solving. They look for problems to fix. Emotions aren't something to be fixed, however, which presents a challenge for technicians. Either they don't have the training to connect with people emotionally, or they don't see it as relevant to their job. Or, even worse, they view emotions as a problem to be solved. Sometimes the most therapeutic intervention is not to fix a problem but to validate the experience.

I often share this with physicians who struggle to deal with the emotional experiences of their patients, and it can apply to any technician. Fix what you can. With the things you can't fix, walk through it with your patient. Long after they forget your technical prowess, they will remember whether you sat with them when they were scared, empathized when they were anxious, walked toward them when things went bad, and celebrated with them when things went well.

For anyone in the healthcare field, I strongly recommend reading Marcus Engle's book *I'm Here: Compassionate Communication in Patient Care*, which chronicles lessons he learned as a patient following a traumatic automobile accident.[3] Many lessons have to do with how we show compassion even when we can't fix everything. These lessons can apply to any leader or organization seeking to improve the customer experience.

Assume Positive Intentions and Check Assumptions

My friend Gloria Cotton, noted expert in diversity, equity, and inclusion, often poses this question to her audiences: "Are you on a treasure hunt or a scavenger hunt?"[4] Scavenger hunters expect to find what's wrong and use it as leverage. Treasure hunters expect to find treasure and affirm it. When we assume negative intentions, our behavior seeks to justify and prove our assumptions. When we assume positive intentions, we look for what's best, real, and true in the other person. We make an effort to take their perspective, put ourselves in their shoes, and test our assumptions before acting on them.

Assuming positive intentions doesn't mean we act blindly or never seek the truth. It means we check assumptions before acting on them. Have you ever felt defensive or angry about something someone said or did? Did you make assumptions about their intent? Maybe you have a history with them. Maybe your own insecurities influenced your conclusion. Regardless, when you act on assumptions, you turn your value switch off for both of you. You don't give them the benefit of the doubt, and you place yourself into a corner without an opportunity to get out.

Here's a template for assuming positive intentions and checking assumptions, especially when you are having a negative reaction:

1.   Identify the behavior to which you are reacting.
2.   Identify the story you are telling yourself and share it with the other person.
3.   Ask whether your story is accurate.

The following are examples of what this looks like:

- "I felt angry when I heard you tell my boss about our conversation. The story I told myself is that you were trying to expose me to make you look better. Was this your intention?"
- "I am so embarrassed. When I arrived late and everyone had already started, the story I told myself was that I'm not needed here. Is that true?"

- "I felt unimportant when you got on your phone while I was talking. The story I told myself is that you aren't that interested in what I have to say. Is this accurate?"
- "I felt angry when I read the comment you posted on my blog. The story I told myself was that you were trying to prove a point and belittle the last person who commented. Was that your intention?"

Sometimes we jump to conclusions about our own value that need to be checked to keep our switch on. If we don't check the validity of our own stories, we can easily fall deeper into a less-than or more-than identity.

The benefits of checking assumptions is that you will usually find the truth and can move forward from there while minimizing destructive behaviors. The challenge is that you might find out you were wrong. Many of us are invested in believing false narratives so we can keep our switches off about ourselves or others. That's not compassion.

When we assume positive intentions and check assumptions, we take ownership over our value and ask others to do the same. These aren't easy conversations to have, but they usually reveal opportunities to talk about what behaviors we could choose instead that would affirm our value.

Affirm Experiences, Even If You Can't Relate

My first rotation as a doctoral psychology intern was at the Veterans Affairs medical center in Tacoma, Washington. I remember it distinctly because of how insufficient I felt that day. I chose a rotation in addiction treatment, so my first assignment was to participate in an addiction recovery group for veterans. Shortly before the first group began, I met with my rotation supervisor, the director of the addiction treatment program. All I remember from that brief meeting was him showing me his clip-on tie and telling me a story of how someone once tried to strangle him with his own necktie. Thankfully, I was wearing a polo shirt.

I joined the circle of chairs, uncertain of how to act, just trying to appear relaxed. As people arrived, their reactions let me know I was definitely an outsider. When the meeting began, my supervisor introduced me to the group and asked me to say a few words about myself. Then, he asked the group if they had any questions for me. The first question came from a grizzly looking middle-aged man with leathery skin and a stringy beard. He asked me, "Are you in recovery? What's your addiction?" I sheepishly disclosed that I was not in recovery but was eager to learn, to which he responded, "Well, then, you can't relate. You have no idea what we are going through."

How do you affirm someone's experience when you can't relate? The good news is that shared experiences aren't a prerequisite. In fact, faking that you understand instead of acknowledging the truth is worse. It's okay to be different, especially if you are trying to be an ally for someone who is in the minority and is experiencing unjust treatment. Here are some ways to affirm someone's experiences even if you haven't been through it yourself:

- "I care about what you are going through."
- "Your experience is valid."
- "I want to learn more about what you are going through."
- "I can't relate, but I want to learn."
- "Will you tell me what it's like to walk in your shoes?"
- "Will you help me understand your experience?"

Being open-minded and curious is extremely helpful when affirming another person's experiences. Even if you can't feel what another person is feeling, you can learn and come to better understand what they're going through. That's called *cognitive empathy*. This can help others feel seen and heard even if you don't have similar experiences and haven't felt what they are feeling.

Empathize by Finding Common Emotional Ground

Have you ever been through something impactful, positive or negative, and not told anyone? Did you carry an emotional burden but nobody knew? Are you currently experiencing something like this and haven't shared it with anyone? I'm certain your friends, family, peers, and employees are also carrying their own burdens.

Emotions are meant to be shared. Without that, we can become lonely, even around others. Over time, we come to believe that nobody else would even understand or that nobody could relate because they haven't been through it. The longer we hide our feelings, the more lonely we get.

Have you ever shared your feelings with someone and found out they were feeling the same way? How did you feel? Relieved? Less alone?

Empathy is about sharing an emotional experience and sending the message to another person, "You aren't alone." Whether we are stirred by another's humanity, or we can actually remember feeling similarly in our own lives, the act of sharing with another person can be transformative. It invites us from a place of *me* or *them* to a place of *we*.

Empathy isn't about having the exact same experience. It's about having a similar emotional response. Maybe you are disappointed about being passed up for a promotion. That hasn't happened to me, but have I ever felt disappointed? Sure. And sharing that is okay. Being disappointed alone is no fun at all. Knowing you aren't the only one who's ever been disappointed somehow makes it a little better. That's the "struggling with" part of compassion.

A fine line exists between empathy and one-upping. Empathy isn't about competing stories. I hate it when I share a struggle or joy that I'm having with my friend, and they take it as an invitation to share a bigger and better story with even more struggle or joy. "You think it's bad getting passed up for a promotion? I got fired from three jobs last month."

One of the reviewers of my book relayed a personal experience with me after reading this section in my draft manuscript. I found it so compelling, relatable, and poignant that I asked her if I could include it. A big thank you to Jennifer for sharing her story and allowing me to share this with you:

> I'm glad you went there. Fear of being "one-upped" is a huge reason why so many people refuse to share. I once served on the board of directors for a nonprofit that provided support and resources for families that had experienced miscarriage, stillbirth, or infant death. There was mutual understanding that, within the behaviors and culture of this organization, we would not value one family's loss over another's. The grief and loss was unique to each family and each situation. The organization would host annual events where structures were in place to honor and support all families in a way that was equitable and individual. Emotions aren't for comparing or out-scoring each other. Emotions are valid, individual, and deeply personal. We can support each other's emotions without judging the value of them.

As soon as you focus on the content of what you went through, you lose connection to the experience of that content. Besides missing the point, when you compete for the better story, you turn your value switch off because you are saying, "My experience is more important than yours." When a person has a hard time showing genuine empathy without focusing on the content of what happened, it usually means their own value switch is off or dimmed. They see empathy as a threat to their own value. If they share in your joy and celebrate your success, then it means they somehow are less than by comparison.

Here are some examples of empathy:

- "I also remember feeling scared when I started my first job."
- "You aren't alone. A lot of people feel that way."
- "I'm with you. That was hard for me too."
- "I'm so happy for you. I remember the joy of a new grandchild."
- "I'm grateful we are going through this together."

Give others the gift of connection by letting them know they aren't alone. The more you can empathize through shared emotional experiences, the greater connection and confidence people around you will have to own, share, and work through their struggles. In a work setting especially, empathy leads to greater connection, which leads to more investment and engagement. Garry Ridge, the CEO of WD-40 who led his company to even more success during the pandemic, puts it this way: "Discretionary effort is inspired by emotional connection at work."[5]

Be Transparent by Sharing Your Own Feelings, Motives, and Experiences

For compassion to work between people, we have to be honest about our feelings, motives, and experiences. Most people aren't. Either we keep our feelings hidden, or we sugarcoat them to avoid dealing with the real stuff. What I didn't share earlier about Bobby Herrera, the cofounder of Populus Group, was the story of his own struggles he didn't want to share with his teammates for many years. As one of thirteen children in a migrant family, he learned the value of hard work, rising early and putting in long hours in the fields. After high school, boot camp became his ticket of opportunity. He is a proud army veteran. Only when he began to share his struggles with his team at Populus Group, however, did he experience the transformational power of transparency. Bobby said, "Only transparency will pay the dividend of stronger connections and shared goals within an organization."[6]

We all have emotional motives, those feeling end states we are secretly pursuing. Maybe I want to feel confident in my role as a new supervisor. Maybe I want to be seen as competent, kind, or knowledgeable. The need to be seen a certain way is a strong emotional motivator, whether we share it or not. We exert a ton of effort every day trying to satisfy these emotional motives, usually without anyone's awareness. And it causes problems. For those wanting to explore this further, I recommend the book *The Anatomy of Peace* by the Arbinger Institute.[7]

This story, shared with me by the assistant to the chief financial officer (CFO) of a large hospital system, illustrates the problem with not sharing our own feelings and motives. The assistant recounted how she had received a request to prepare several financial documents for the CFO but didn't know why. She prepared the documents and sent them to her boss. The next day, the CFO asked her to run the reports again but with a few slightly different angles. She wondered why this was necessary but didn't question it. It seemed unnecessary to the assistant, and she felt a little resentful for having to spend the extra time.

The next day, the CFO asked again, this time for several more reports. This time the assistant felt quite burdened having to take more of her valuable time doing what seemed like duplicative work. She didn't want to question her boss, but she also wanted to know what was going on, so she mustered up her courage and called her boss, asking what was going on. The CFO fumbled around for a bit, getting defensive at first, but eventually revealed the truth. She revealed that she was preparing for a big presentation to the board of directors and was anxious. She kept second-guessing herself, trying to anticipate what they might ask and wanted to feel confident going into the meeting.

The assistant explained her response to learning this from her boss: "Why didn't she just tell me that up front? I would have gladly helped her. I don't want my boss to be unprepared or embarrassed. I would have been much more willing to give energy to this project if I had known why it mattered to her."

How can people struggle with you if they don't know what you are struggling with?

Doug Conant, a leadership expert and the CEO who turned around Campbell Soup Company, learned that when you get vulnerable, people pay more attention, not less. This enables performance to transcend the ordinary because people struggle together toward a common goal instead of trying to read minds, feeling resentful, or overcompensating.

Marlene Chism has written an excellent book about healthy conflict titled *From Conflict to Courage*.[8] In my conversation with her, one of her main assertions is that most conflict arises from conversations we should have had but didn't.[9] In her experience, most people aren't honest about how they feel or what they want, but these feelings and thoughts are critical for strong, trusting relationships. In fact, emotional awareness and intelligence are important, she says, "but integrity means taking ownership for your feelings, interpretations, and experiences."

Here are some examples of sharing feelings, motives, and experiences:

- "I'm anxious about being able to lead my team remotely right now."
- "I've noticed I'm not sleeping as well because I keep replaying past conversations in my head."
- "I want to be respected by my executive team."
- "I'm excited about our upcoming merger."
- "I'm worried about how our product launch will reflect on me as a leader. I want it to go well."

A leader's internal emotional world is an important part of who they are, and it influences them in so many ways. When leaders get honest about what's going on inside, they experience higher levels of engagement, support, and teamwork.

Embrace Vulnerability

Vulnerability is indeed a secret weapon but only under one condition: when transparency is not viewed as a weakness. The only way to disconnect the two is to recognize *your value as a human being is not dependent on how others respond to you. Your value comes from within you, not from how others perceive you.*

Adam Grant, noted organizational psychologist and bestselling author, articulates this idea so well: "Vulnerability is not the opposite of resilience. Vulnerability builds resilience. Projecting perfection protects your ego but shuts people out and stunts your growth. Revealing struggles shows humility and humanity, opening the door to new sources of support and strength."[10]

Trust is a central theme for most of the leaders and teams with whom we work. They want more of it, so we ask them what trust means to them. I like to ask leaders this question: "What would it take for you to trust someone?" With few exceptions, they will answer by listing behaviors they expect from the other person. This other person must be reliable, maintain privacy of sensitive information, follow through on promises, and not use personal information against them. Rarely does anyone describe what they themselves would need to do to trust another person.

This understanding of trust is one-sided, as if the other person is completely responsible for earning trust and the leader is a passive benefactor of those trust-building behaviors.

Let's focus specifically on trust behaviors that have a personal, emotional impact. These could include disclosing personal information to a third party when it was supposed to be private, using something shared in confidence against the person to spite or hurt them, or even unintentional slips that feel like betrayal. In most of these cases, it's normal to feel embarrassed, exposed, or defensive—in short, vulnerable.

If you don't want to feel vulnerable, then it might make sense to avoid trusting anyone. Except leaders can't succeed if they never trust anyone or expect people to meet unrealistic behavioral standards before they open up. Some leaders can make this leap, some can't. The difference lies in how they view their own value.

Leaders who keep their value switch on recognize that betrayal hurts but that they are still okay. They embrace the vulnerability of being open with their people, fully acknowledging the risk but knowing that how people respond to them doesn't define them. When they feel angry, exposed, embarrassed, or defensive, they share it, work through it, and seek new commitments going forward.

This type of vulnerability requires the boundary of not letting another person's perceptions and reactions define us. As Gandhi allegedly said, "I will not let anyone walk through my mind with their dirty feet."

Leaders who let their value switch turn off see vulnerability as a threat to their own identity. They respond in one of two ways: don't trust anyone, or, when trust is broken, attack themselves or the other person for it. Without taking responsibility for their emotions, they don't assert their own value, and they don't engage the other person to do the same. They see breaches of trust as validation to turn the value switch off or keep it off.

Amy Balog, an executive coach to leaders who are struggling to find their bearings in seemingly impossible corporate situations, believes that leaders must take personal responsibility for their vulnerability instead of leaving it in someone else's hands.[11] She distinguishes between a safeguarded heart and an unsheltered heart. A safeguarded heart means I am okay and protected not because of the circumstances around me but because I am capable of taking the next step and owning my inherent value. An unsheltered heart means that I am fully exposed because my worth is up for grabs at any moment. A safeguarded heart can be vulnerable without turning off the value switch.

Remember That You Don't Have to Agree with Someone to Value Them as a Person

If you pay any attention to politics, social media, or the news, you probably wonder if anyone is able to disagree respectfully anymore. Everything seems to get politicized and polarized so quickly. Cancel culture is a great example. When people disagree with someone's views on something, they immediately turn off their value switch. "You aren't valuable if you don't agree with me." Social media is even worse.

I've been blogging for almost ten years. One post has received more attention than any other.[12] It started as a feel-good story about my daughter, who worked in customer service at a big-box home improvement store. People are usually grateful for her help, and they usually use one of two phrases to express it: "I appreciate it" or "I appreciate you." She noticed that "I appreciate you" was much more impactful to her and meant a lot more to her than "I appreciate it." I posted this story and asked people to weigh in on their favorite, posing this as an example of different strokes for different folks. I invited people to try both phrases, see what results they got, and share their experiences in the comments.

If you look at this post now, you won't see many comments on it. That's because of how ugly it got. I blocked some of the comments that were submitted because they were so hateful. I have no problem with people weighing in, sharing their perspectives, even telling what happened when they tried it. But I got comments dismissing anyone who disagreed, making racial generalizations, and attacking the opposite view. I was shocked how many comments revealed that the writer had their value switch turned off.

You might argue that my choice to block these comments meant that I didn't value those contributors whose comments I didn't like. Perhaps, although I see it as me setting boundaries around maintaining the value of all people impacted by what I post on my blog. They are okay, but their comments are not okay.

One thing that made Abraham Lincoln such a great leader was that he surrounded himself with people who had different views, even people he had run against and beat in elections. He valued alternate perspectives and recognized that diversity of ideas and views is what makes a team—and nation—strong. The relationship between US Supreme Court Justices Ruth Bader Ginsburg and Antonin Scalia is a great example of keeping the value switch on even during disagreement. Although they had different legal positions on most issues, they were close friends and had a deep respect for each other.

Leaders who encourage different viewpoints and stay curious are able to benefit from the wealth of experience on their teams and find better solutions to problems.

Separate the Person from the Behavior

Have you ever dreaded a performance conversation? Do you take feedback about your performance personally? Do you struggle to give corrective feedback to employees because they might take it personally?

Compassion is about getting personal without making it personal. With the value switch off, conversations about performance or behavior are often interpreted as judgments about a person's worth. With the value switch on, we can have personal and candid conversations about behavior without implicating a person's worth as a human.

This doesn't mean these conversations are easy. It stings to be told that our behavior didn't measure up or that we let someone down. It's uncomfortable talking about performance or behavior gaps with employees. It can be done, though, while keeping our value switch on. To do this, we must follow two important principles.

First, focus on behavior and avoid assumptions about character or intentions. When confronting behavior, describe the behavior itself, the expectations or standards, and the impact it had on the team or organization. Don't make assumptions about a person's intentions or character. Table 4.2 shows some examples.

The second principle for having productive performance conversations is to avoid the trap of trying to manage other people's feelings. You are responsible for your feelings and behaviors, not theirs. Talking about behavior and performance gaps is hard, and it invites uncomfortable feelings. This is normal and okay. But if leaders try to protect themselves or others from these feelings, they will lose objectivity

TABLE 4.2. Examples illustrating the difference between confronting behavior and questioning a person's intentions or character

Confronting behaviors	Questioning a person's intentions or character
"You have failed to meet your sales quota for three consecutive months."	"You're slacking. What's wrong with you?"
"That comment was inappropriate. Will you apologize to the client?"	"What were you thinking? Why were you trying to sabotage our sale?"
"I forgot to include you in the meeting invite, and I'm sorry. I'll send you the minutes."	"I'm so forgetful, I always mess things up."
"I'm angry. We agreed on your role in the meeting, and you didn't follow through."	"You really disappointed me. I expected more from you."
"I failed."	"I'm such a failure."
"This is the third time you've been late. What's getting in your way?"	"You are always late. Why can't you step up?"

and compromise their duty. I've seen too many leaders beat around the bush, avoid tough conversations, or fall all over themselves trying to soften the message to avoid hurt feelings. Keeping our value switch on during difficult conversations means recognizing that strong emotions are a normal part of the process. Because we care about others and accept their emotions as legitimate, we don't need to manage those emotions.

Do leaders care about how others feel? Of course they do. Are they responsible for other people's feelings? No. They are responsible for being honest, supportive, and consistent.

Include and Leverage Diversity

Compassion views diversity as an opportunity. I truly believe that diversity is part of the grand design of the universe. Science shows us that diversity is the key to flourishing. It's also the source of conflict. Conflict usually arises out of difference. It's human nature to be suspicious of what's unfamiliar and what we don't understand. It takes effort to overcome our human nature and recognize that diversity is a gift to be leveraged, not minimized. It means we have to learn how to utilize the energy of conflict to create instead of destroy. However you are approaching diversity, equity, and inclusion in your organization, I encourage you to take the next step and view diversity as an asset and opportunity.

Tolerating differences is the lowest common denominator. Putting up with things you don't understand and don't like is about as basic as you can get: "I can't stand you, but at least I don't trip you when you walk past my cubicle."

The next step is celebrating diversity. Here, we look for the beauty in diversity and acknowledge it. That's an improvement over tolerance because at least we are looking for the positives. For example, your company has an ethnic luncheon. Everyone brings food from their culture. "That's great," you say, "but let's not forget why we are here—to get stuff done and make a difference in the world." Celebrating diversity still isn't enough.

Leveraging diversity is when we make the big step to accept that diversity is necessary to our survival and is the key to thriving teams, communities, and organizations.

If inclusion means you are working to make sure everyone is heard, affirmed, invited, and included, that's a great place to start. But what if you looked deeper? What if you looked for the unique qualities in each person that could be leveraged to advance the organization? What if you viewed differences as assets that have a purpose and role to create what's next? When our value switch is on, we go beyond tolerating and celebrating. We actively search out and utilize diversity to make us better.

When leaders practice these nine behaviors, it promotes safe and welcoming work cultures where value is affirmed and differences are leveraged for the good of the whole.

But use caution! The value switch is only one of three switches that make up the compassion mindset. It cannot stand alone. Without the switches of capability and responsibility, value won't be able to find the wisdom or courage necessary to truly struggle with the self and others through the biggest challenges. Value is the foundation and prerequisite for Compassionate Accountability, but for energy to flow freely, the other two switches must also be on. Keep reading to learn about the next switch.

Main Points

The main points of this chapter are summarized in table 4.3.

Turn on your value switch with these nine behaviors:

- Listen to and validate feelings without judging.
- Assume positive intentions and check assumptions.

TABLE 4.3. Summary of the differences when a value switch is off versus on

Value switch is off	Value switch is on
Emotions are a liability and should be kept out of workplace relationships.	Emotions are valid and a critical component of workplace relationships.
Vulnerability is a sign of weakness.	Vulnerability is a sign of courage and humility.
Human worth is measured by performance.	Human worth is not measured, it is innate.
Differences, disagreements, and diversity are threats to be minimized.	Differences, disagreements, and diversity are opportunities to be leveraged.

- Affirm experiences, even if you can't relate.
- Empathize by finding common emotional ground.
- Be transparent by sharing your own feelings, motives, and experiences.
- Embrace vulnerability.
- Remember that you don't have to agree with someone to value them as a person.
- Separate the person from the behavior.
- Include and leverage diversity.

Quiz Answers

Table 4.4 shows the answers to the value switch interactions quiz in table 4.1.

TABLE 4.4. Answers to the value switch interactions quiz

What you observe	Is the value switch on? Y/N
1. Your gut tells you something's not right. You decide to speak up even though you are unsure how it will be received.	Y
2. You ask someone how they are coping with a difficult change at work, and they respond, "You gotta do what you gotta do."	N
3. You ask your boss to help you deal with a coworker who seems to be sabotaging your efforts on the team. She responds by telling you, "He's just jealous."	N
4. Someone confides in you about a challenge, and you tell them about a bigger challenge you had, reassuring them, "It could be worse."	N
5. You appropriately confront an employee about a performance problem, and she responds by saying, "I don't feel safe right now."	N
6. You confront the most assertive person in the meeting and ask them to stop interrupting so your more introverted peer can finish what she was saying.	Y
7. You share a concern with your boss about a coworker's behavior, and he responds, "Why are you getting so upset?"	N
8. You are a white American male, and your coworker is a female from India. You ask her, "I feel awkward because I don't always know how I come across to you."	Y

Commentary on Quiz Answers

Let's explore the value switch interaction quiz answers from table 4.4 in more depth.

1. Your gut instinct is an important internal indicator of how you are doing. It's important and necessary to listen to your gut. Speaking up is often difficult, especially when we aren't sure how people will respond. Giving voice to our feelings is one way we keep our own value switch on. Sharing how you are feeling doesn't guarantee you will get what you want or that people will respond as you wish. But it does guarantee that you have appropriately honored your own internal experience. Did you know that most airline accidents are caused by someone's gut instinct getting ignored? In most cases, somebody knew something that didn't feel right. They either didn't say anything or tried to say something and were shut down. You never know; that feeling you have inside might help you avoid a bigger accident later.

2. There's nothing wrong with caring about your coworker. Reaching out when you sense they are struggling is a compassionate thing to do. In this situation, the person refused to open up and avoided sharing their feelings by redirecting the conversation to *what* they are doing, rather than *how*. This person had their value switch off and avoided your offer for support.

   If your coworker's value switch were on, they might have responded, "Thanks so much for asking. I've been feeling _____."

3. Your boss's value switch was off for your coworker because she led with an assumption that his behavior was caused by him being jealous of you.

If your boss's value switch were on, she might have said, "I'm sorry you are experiencing this. How can I help?"

4. Responding to someone else's story with a worse story of your own is an example of one-upping masquerading as empathy coupled with minimizing another person's experience. They don't need you to share your bigger and better story. And telling them "It could be worse" doesn't address how they are actually experiencing their situation right now. You may think you are doing them a favor by offering perspective, but the most helpful thing you could do is listen and validate what they are going through without comparing it to anything.

    If your value switch were on, you might say something such as "I appreciate you trusting me to share this. I'm here to listen and support you."

5. Your employee responding to your appropriate feedback with "I don't feel safe right now" is an example of emotional hijacking. Your employee is using a charged emotional statement to push you away and avoid accountability. This scenario assumes that you *appropriately* confronted your employee about their performance problem. This means you focused on the behavior, didn't make it personal, and did not confront them in a discriminatory way. In situations like this, we need to recognize that people may bring contextual and other factors into the situation. Maybe your employee has felt unsafe in previous situations like this and assumes this will be the same. Maybe they confuse the conflict of accountability with a personal attack. Or maybe they have learned that when they turn up the emotional heat, people back off and don't hold them accountable.

    If your employee's value switch were on, she might say something like, "I feel defensive and don't know how to respond. May I ask some clarifying questions to be sure I understand your concern?" Or if she is worried about being treated unfairly and wants to check assumptions, she might say, "I am feeling defensive right now. The story I am telling myself is that I am being held to a different standard because of my race. Is this accurate?"

6. You took action to make space for your more introverted peer—well done! That took courage for you to speak up and be an ally for your coworker. When we use our voice to help let others' voices be heard, that's called *advocacy*. In doing so, you also reinforced that message that everyone's voice deserves to be heard.

7. Your boss has his value switch off for you. The way he asked the question "Why are you getting so upset?" implies he thinks your experience isn't credible or valid. It's appropriate and important for your boss to find out what's going on but not with a minimizing response like this.

    If your boss's value switch were on, he might say something like, "I can tell you are upset, and I'm here to listen. Will you share more with me about what's going on?"

8. It takes humility to share your own vulnerability and admit your blind spots, especially in high-risk situations for unconscious bias. When your value switch is on, you are willing to get vulnerable to show respect and open yourself up to what you might be missing.

CHAPTER 5

THE CAPABILITY SWITCH

THE SECOND SWITCH of the compassion mindset is the switch of capability. When the switch is on, we believe and behave in ways that affirm capability and contribution are possible. When the switch is off, we believe capability is limited and behave in ways that reinforce that belief, as shown in figure 5.1.

FIGURE 5.1. The capability switch.
Designed by Scott Light, CG Studios.

Turning on the capability switch involves the fundamental belief that anyone can be part of the solution.

What does this mean? Our unique qualities, skills, and experiences deserve to be affirmed, and we deserve the opportunity to contribute, learn, and grow in a collaborative environment.

Here's a short quiz to test your understanding of this switch. Using this initial definition of what it means to have our capability switch on, evaluate the interactions listed in table 5.1. The correct answers are at the end of this chapter in table 5.3, along with commentary to help with deeper understanding and application.

When the Capability Switch Is Off

When the capability switch is turned off, we view capability as limited or stagnant. We see barriers instead of opportunity. We nurture beliefs such as "You'd never understand" or "You don't have the proper education to grasp this." We expect people to prove themselves before we trust them or believe in them. We take failure as a sign to abandon ship or give up.

Four clusters of behaviors let us know that the capability switch is off:

- Getting attached to our own solutions
- Having a scarcity mindset
- Avoiding investing in people
- Controlling information and resources

Getting Attached to Our Own Solutions

When our capability switch is off, we get invested in our own ideas. We cling to having our ideas recognized rather than looking for the best solution among many. This happens because our identity is wrapped

TABLE 5.1. Capability switch interactions quiz

What you observe	Is the capability switch on? Y/N
1. You hear someone say, "You can't fix stupid."	_____
2. The unwritten rule is "Never admit you don't know something."	_____
3. Your supervisor asks a lot of curious questions and shows genuine interest in your ideas.	_____
4. Your boss says, "Failure is not an option."	_____
5. You take the time to notice the positive attributes and contributions of others.	_____
6. Your team motto is "The best idea wins."	_____
7. It seems like whoever talks the most gets rewarded.	_____
8. During orientation, your department director shares her philosophy that learning from mistakes is a fundamental aspect of success.	_____

up in being heard and recognized for our ideas. Our ego convinces us that getting credit is important, so we get attached to our own solutions, seeking first to be understood rather than to understand. This shows up in behaviors such as arguing for our own ideas, dismissing others' ideas, and continuing to advocate for our idea even when it's not the best solution for the team. In some work cultures, people are rewarded for knowing the answer instead of helping others learn and grow. Leaders seek to be solution boards rather than sounding boards.

Having a Scarcity Mindset

A second set of behaviors is motivated by a scarcity mindset. Seeing resources as limited, we clamor for our piece of the pie, worry about getting enough resources for our teams, and complain when we don't think we are treated fairly. With a scarcity mindset, leaders see limitations and obstacles instead of opportunities. They focus on what can't be done, what's getting in the way, and what will go wrong. Failure is seen as an indictment of their value, so avoiding failure becomes a priority. Seeing the glass as half-empty, they infect their teams with pessimism and negativity. Innovation suffers, and people play it safe instead of taking healthy risks and learning from mistakes.

Avoiding Investing in People

Another cluster of behaviors that turn off the capability switch involves avoiding investing in people. For a variety of reasons, we decide that building capacity is not worth it. We make excuses such as "I'm too busy," "You wouldn't understand anyway," "You should be grateful to have a job," or "You won't be around long enough for us to get a return on our investment." The busier we are, the easier it is to focus on production at the expense of building production capacity. We choose short-term gain in exchange for long-term pain in the form of stagnation and inertia. Engagement and retention suffer because people aren't learning and growing.

Controlling Information and Resources

When our capability switch is off, information and resources are used to gain power rather than to empower. We hold on to information that might give us an advantage. Sharing resources that could help others is seen as a threat to our position. Leaders who control information and resources would rather have a personal advantage than help others succeed. As a result, people are deprived of resources that could make a difference, collaboration is squashed, and performance suffers.

The result of having our capability switch off is an environment that lacks curiosity and where innovation and creativity suffer. People aren't included or challenged, and engagement drops.

Leaders whose capability switch is off are what bestselling author Liz Wiseman calls *diminishers*.[1] They treat employees as resources to be deployed and left to languish. The opposite are *multipliers*, leaders whose capability switch is on and who multiply talent, generating up to two times more productivity.

Turn On Your Capability Switch

Because people are capable, everyone deserves the invitation to contribute, participate, take ownership, and be part of the solution.

Here are five behavioral strategies that help leaders turn on, and keep on, their capability switch:

- Seek first to understand.
- Share ideas and resources to find the best solutions.
- Invite people to be part of the solution.
- Invest in each other's success.
- Turn failures into learning opportunities.

Seek First to Understand

Everyone has experienced that person who doesn't actually listen. While you are talking, they are thinking of what they want to say next. If they ask any questions, it's only to tee up their own conversation topic. They are quick to judge and slow to listen.

Compassion allows us to suspend judgment in place of curiosity. When our capability switch is on, we take time to learn about people's experiences, skills, and gifts. We ask curious questions and listen openly to the answer. Even if we can't relate, we seek to understand a person's perspective by asking them what it's like to be in their shoes.

My wife and I play a little game at family reunions. We keep track of how many relatives we interact with are actually curious. We consider a relative to be curious if they ask more than one question in a row. If they ask a question only to turn the conversation back on themselves, they aren't curious. If they ask at least one more follow-up question and seem interested in learning more, they are curious. More than two questions and the conversation starts to be enjoyable because we feel seen and heard. We make it a goal to practice this kind of curiosity in each of our interactions.

Making assumptions about a person's motives is a great way to turn off your capability switch. Seeking first to understand means testing our own assumptions about others to be sure we aren't heading down the wrong path. The previous chapter offered a template for how to do this.

Communication gaps are one of the biggest demotivators within toxic workplaces. Closing the gap starts with asking your employees what they need to do their jobs better. This may not be the same as what you think is important or what you think they need. Marlene Chism, a leadership and workplace conflict expert, encourages leaders to stop playing "power of attorney" and stop speaking for others and instead let them own their experience, needs, and wants.[2] This is the best way to truly learn how you can best help them.

Share Ideas and Resources to Find the Best Solutions

Millie Ward is the president of Stone Ward, a full-service marketing agency based in Little Rock, Arkansas. In 2019 Stone Ward was named one of *Inc.* magazine's best places to work. Building capability is the key to engagement at Stone Ward, and creativity is the key to their success with clients, which is why I love this quote from Millie about how Stone Ward approaches the creative process: *"A good idea doesn't care who had it!"*

Stone Ward truly embodies the philosophy that the best solutions come when people share ideas and drop their egos. Never withhold information that might help someone.

How do leaders build cultures in which ideas are shared and the best solutions emerge? Surely if leaders invite input, that's sufficient, right? Karin Hurt and David Dye argue otherwise. They are the founders of Let's Grow Leaders, a firm dedicated to this very idea. In their book *Courageous Cultures: How to Build Teams of Microinnovators, Problem Solvers, and Customer Advocates*, they argue that having an open-door policy isn't enough.[3] Leaders must take the next step to turn on and keep on the capability switch.

David and Karin suggest a three-step plan for how to respond when someone comes to you with an idea. First, respond with gratitude. Thank the person for their courage and willingness to come forward with their idea. Second, share any relevant information you have that might impact their idea. As a leader, you might know facts that could make a difference. Third, invite their participation going forward. Engaging people to be part of the solution is the essence of capability. David and Karin have seen this three-step process not only cultivate curiosity but also build and maintain momentum for courageous cultures that share ideas and resources to find the best solutions.

In the Tao Te Ching, Lao-Tzu writes, "The sage does not hoard, and thereby bestows. The more one lives for others, the greater his life. The more one gives to others, the greater his abundance."

Invite People to Be Part of the Solution

Under Garry Ridge's leadership, WD-40 Company thrived and grew stronger during the COVID-19 pandemic. In my conversation with Garry, he credited this to the company culture that was able to pivot around fear.[4] I asked Garry the secret to his success, and he shared with me that the three most powerful words he has learned to use are "I don't know."

Why is this phrase so powerful? First, it shows humility. Garry was clear that he doesn't know all the answers. Especially during a crisis, leaders can't possibly have it all figured out. Acting like they do is hubris and a setup for failure. Garry believes that leadership is about staying curious, getting comfortable with ambiguity, and being a lifelong learner. Second, by not trying to have all the answers, Garry invites others to be part of the solution. By saying, "I don't know," he empowers others to step up and participate.

Blaine Bartlett is the president and CEO of Avatar Resources Inc. and founder of the compassionate capitalism movement. His work is focused on the thesis that business, as the most pervasive force on the planet, is charged with taking responsibility for the well-being of the whole.[5] Keeping with the theme that compassion is a process of struggling with, Blaine is a big believer in the power of inviting people into the process. *"Without cocreation, all you have is compliance. Cocreation transfers ownership and increases positive stewardship of our resources,"* Blaine argues. Unless leaders create movement through cocreation, it will eventually devolve into self-interest.

When leaders have their capability switch on, they are continually looking for ways to include others in the process. The more others participate, the more ownership they have. The more they contribute, the more capable they feel. And, for the leader, it transforms the struggle and shares the load.

Invest in Each Other's Success

Capability is enhanced when we invest in the success of others. That's one of the most important roles of a leader. Bobby Herrera, the CEO of Populus Group, embodies this philosophy. Bobby encourages leaders to learn the best way to communicate with every person so they can find ways to stretch their potential without overwhelming them. Challenge people to do more than they believe they are capable of. His philosophy is best captured by this mantra: "Want more for your people than you want from them."

What a fantastic philosophy. When we want more for our people than we want from them, we can truly invest in them beyond their immediate contribution to the organization. We can ask them to step up and become more because we believe in them.

Larry Carlson helped build HBO into one of the largest cable subscription channels in the world. He did this by investing in the success of his people. I asked him about his philosophy of leadership, and he told me, "Your employees may be working for you on paper, but you should be working for them in reality." The best leaders succeed by helping their people succeed. As leaders, we owe our people the support and inspiration to be their best and benefit others.[6]

Turn Failures into Learning Opportunities

When I was a ropes-course facilitator, I worked with teams seeking to build trust and cohesion by engaging them in various problem-solving activities. I remember one group in particular whose leader had her capability switch off. The group had struggled valiantly on one element of the ropes course and had not accomplished the goal they set for themselves. We were debriefing the activity, and I asked about how they felt about failing to reach their goal. The leader interrupted me to remind me, "We don't use the word *failure*." As we explored her comment and continued processing with the group, I realized that this team didn't have a tool kit for dealing with failure. They didn't want to face their feelings about it and had settled on just avoiding the conversation. Consequently, they weren't open to the question "What can we learn from our failures?"

Pretending that we don't fail is on one end of the spectrum. The other end is illustrated by the statement "Failure isn't an option." This philosophy suggests that failure is a bad thing to be avoided at all costs.

Either way, failure is seen as the enemy, something we want to avoid or not talk about.

Failure isn't the problem. Failure is normal. Failure happens many times each day when we don't reach our goals, don't follow through on a commitment, or come up short despite our best efforts. Failure is a terrific teacher if we allow it. Knowing what didn't work is helpful going forward. When our capability switch is on, we don't fear failure, because it's not an indictment of our value or capability. In fact, it's a gift and an invitation to increase our capability.

Self-efficacy is a person's belief in their ability to mobilize the resources necessary to meet the demands they experience. Self-efficacy is a strong predictor of performance and resilience and is backed by over forty years of social-science research.[7] Self-efficacy research shows that role models have an impact on whether a person feels more or less confident to mobilize their own response to various demands. Coping role models, who aren't perfect and learn from mistakes, have a much stronger positive impact than perfection role models, those who never make a mistake. You are unlikely to gain self-efficacy by watching a video of Tiger Woods making a perfect putt. But learning about the obstacles he overcame and how he picked himself up after setbacks gives every young golfer the belief that he's been in their shoes. This is what gets them up every day. Coping models are relatable. It's not about how often or how spectacularly you fail but how quickly you get up and make corrections.

Laura Cole, founder of Your Latitude, a Canadian solution-focused coaching and mediation practice, specializes in organizational culture development and change management. She encourages leaders to reorient a team's curiosity to focus on how they want the future to look different rather than rehashing the past. This attitude helps build capability by asking, "What could be different and better next time?" rather than being inhibited by past failures. It also helps share responsibility for what's next rather than pointing fingers, which we'll get to in the next chapter.

Here are some tips to help turn failure into learning opportunities:

- Support and validate the difficult emotions that come with failure—sadness, loss, embarrassment, anger, anxiety. These are all normal and okay to talk about. We are human.
- Avoid pointing fingers. Instead of asking, "Who did it?" ask, "What didn't work?"
- Separate the person from the mistake. We might have failed, but we aren't a failure.
- Distill key learnings. Ask, "What did we learn from this?"
- Encourage people to share their stories of failure and overcoming obstacles. Ask, "When have you failed, and how did you learn from it?"
- If the mistake or failure resulted in harm, make amends. Ask, "What do we need to do to make amends for what happened?"
- If the stakes are high and consequences for failing again are significant, work to mitigate risk and increase the chance of success. Ask, "What can we do to increase our level of confidence going forward?"
- Celebrate success. Failure is hard, so make sure to notice and celebrate successes as well.
- Cocreate your preferred future. Use mistakes as inspiration to design a different outcome next time.

These five behavior clusters turn on and keep on the capability switch to promote a curious, collaborative, and inclusive environment where people feel empowered to be part of the solution. This is the second of three switches that all work together and must be turned on to practice Compassionate Accountability.

Main Points

The main points of this chapter are summarized in table 5.2.

Turn on your capability switch with these five behaviors:

- Seek first to understand.
- Share ideas and resources to find the best solutions.
- Invite people to be part of the solution.
- Invest in each other's success.
- Turn failure into learning opportunities.

TABLE 5.2. Summary of the differences when a capability switch is off versus on

Capability switch is off	Capability switch is on
Seek first to be understood.	Seek first to understand.
Control and fight over resources (scarcity mindset).	Share resources (abundance mindset).
Assume others can't or won't help solve the problem.	Invite people to be part of the solution.
Avoid investing in people.	Want more for your people than you want from them.
Mistakes are to be avoided. Failure is not an option.	Mistakes are opportunities to learn and grow. Failure is the best teacher.

Quiz Answers

Table 5.3 shows the answers to the capability switch interaction quiz in table 5.1.

TABLE 5.3. Answers to the capability switch interactions quiz

What you observe	Is the capability switch on? Y/N
1. You hear someone say, "You can't fix stupid."	N
2. The unwritten rule is "Never admit you don't know something."	N
3. Your supervisor asks a lot of curious questions and shows genuine interest in your ideas.	Y
4. Your boss says, "Failure is not an option."	N
5. You take the time to notice the positive attributes and contributions of others.	Y
6. Your team motto is "The best idea wins."	Y
7. It seems like whoever talks the most gets rewarded.	N
8. During orientation, your department director shares her philosophy that learning from mistakes is a fundamental aspect of success.	Y

Commentary on Quiz Answers

Let's explore the capability switch interaction quiz answers from table 5.3 in more depth.

1. This may seem obvious, but even joking statements such as "You can't fix stupid" reveal a person who has their capability switch turned off. This attitude implies that some people can't learn and grow.

    If this person had their capability switch turned on, they might say something such as "She's struggling to learn this new skill. I wonder what else we could try to help her figure it out."

2. Being afraid to admit you don't know something is a sign of either a fragile ego, a toxic work environment, or both. And this fear is one of the biggest threats to innovation. Many of our training programs involve periodic quizzes to test comprehension along the way. It's critical that I can check where people are at to adjust pace and approach for maximum learning. My rules when reviewing quiz results are (1) I trust you to grade your own quiz, and (2) if you missed an answer, I ask you to share it with the group and seek help from others until you understand the rationale behind the right answer. I do this to reinforce a learning culture where learning from mistakes is normal and safe.

    If the capability switch was turned on in this work culture, the rule would be explicit, such as "If you don't know something, it's okay to speak up because we want to help you learn and grow."

3. Inviting input and showing genuine interest in your employees' ideas will help generate better solutions, foster greater engagement, and ensure buy-in when it counts the most. If you believe your people are your greatest asset, this is how you demonstrate it.

4. Let's be honest, failure is always an option, albeit one we don't like. It stings and feels vulnerable and embarrassing. But it doesn't make us less worthy as a human. After a monumental comeback, I've heard coaches and athletes explain their efforts by saying, "I hate losing more than I love winning." Instead of making failure the bad guy, these winners use the feeling of failure to motivate them toward what they want instead.

    With our capability switches on, we might chant, "Failure sucks. Success rocks. This is why we squeeze every last bit of intelligence from our failures and turn them into stepping stones for success."

5. You get more of what you pay attention to. An abundance mindset is not threatened by the success of others. Just the opposite. By noticing the good that others bring, you will get more of it. Not only that, but you are cultivating your own practice of gratitude for the amazing talent you have on your team.

6. I once heard Millie Ward, founding owner of Stone Ward, say it best: "The best idea doesn't care who had it." Seeking the best solution instead of our own solutions shows that you are committed to the team and organization's success rather than your own ego.

7. Who can relate to the dynamic that the most talkative person gets rewarded? Who can't relate! Nothing is more frustrating and demotivating to the brilliant introverts and considerate listeners than when the loud talkers and conversation dominators get all the attention. It's as if volume and quantity is associated with being more capable and competent. We all know this isn't true. Sadly, cultures favoring outspoken people is a form of discrimination that undermines confidence and contribution from the rest. In the quiz from the previous chapter, a courageous teammate with her value switch on spoke up to interrupt a meeting dominator and gave her introverted peer a chance to talk. Sometimes that's what it takes to keep the lights on.

8. Your department director is encouraging capability by framing failure as an opportunity to learn and grow. In chapter 8, I share a case study about a hospital that is replacing progressive discipline with Compassionate Accountability as a strategy to pursue high reliability. The leadership team recognizes that the key to reducing errors is to learn and grow from mistakes as fast as possible, and this requires a safe and collaborative environment.

CHAPTER 6

THE RESPONSIBILITY SWITCH

THE THIRD SWITCH of the compassion mindset is the switch of responsibility. When the switch is on, we believe and behave in ways that share responsibility for outcomes. When the switch is off, we believe that responsibility should be isolated and behave in ways to reinforce that belief, as shown in figure 6.1.

FIGURE 6.1. The responsibility switch.
Designed by Scott Light, CG Studios.

Turning on the responsibility switch involves the fundamental belief that *everyone is responsible for their own thoughts, feelings, and actions.*

What does this mean? We are responsible for only our own thoughts, feelings, and behaviors, not those of others. Regardless of what happened before, we are each 100 percent responsible for what we do next. No more, no less.

Table 6.1 includes a short quiz to test your understanding of this switch. Using this initial definition of what it means to have our responsibility switch on, evaluate the following interactions. The correct answers are at the end of this chapter in table 6.5, along with commentary to help with deeper understanding and application.

When the Responsibility Switch Is Off

When our responsibility switch is off, we lose track of the fundamental truth that we cannot control others, but we can control our own responses. In an effort to mask our discomfort or inadequacies and avoid difficult conversations, we isolate responsibility in ways that get us further away from real solutions. When our responsibility switch is off, we forget or abandon the boundaries about who's responsible for what.

These five clusters of observable behaviors let us know the responsibility switch is off:

- Avoiding taking responsibility for our own feelings, thoughts, or behaviors
- Taking over responsibility for others' feelings, thoughts, or behaviors
- Attacking or blaming to isolate responsibility
- Turning conflict into a win-or-lose power struggle
- Focusing on self-preservation and self-promotion

TABLE 6.1. Responsibility switch interactions quiz

What you observe	Is the responsibility switch on? Y/N
1. When you make a mistake, you own it, apologize, and make it right.	_____
2. Your coworker says, "The way you talked to that customer made everyone so embarrassed."	_____
3. You tell your work partner, "We agreed to complete the list by the weekend. You can count on me to do my part."	_____
4. Your boss seems to have high expectations because you're always coming up short, but you don't have direct conversations about what they are.	_____
5. After your friend makes a critical mistake, you say, "What can you do differently so this doesn't happen again?"	_____
6. Personal gain takes priority over team or company goals.	_____
7. You make a mistake, and your coworker says to you, "You made your bed, now you have to lie in it."	_____
8. Someone says, "I feel embarrassed. It's not okay to talk to customers like that."	_____

Avoiding Taking Responsibility for Our Own Feelings, Thoughts, or Behaviors

Isolating responsibility can mean taking on too much or too little ownership for our own feelings, thoughts, and behaviors. This might be one of the most challenging aspects of being a leader and the area where we see the most confusion, so this section includes a lot more detail.

When we take on too little responsibility, we avoid owning the parts that are only ours to own. Our behaviors indicate a bid for others to take over responsibility so we don't have to. Consider these five statements, each of them reflecting a responsibility switch turned off.

- "That really made me upset."
- "You disrespected me."
- "It's not my fault that I didn't have the instructions in advance."
- "I expected more from you, you let me down."
- "If you do that again, I'll have no choice but to fire you."

In table 6.2, I've explained the bid to avoid responsibility and the compassionate truth that is being avoided.

Here's another example illustrated through a common scenario. In advance of an important executive team meeting, you sent out an email to the team with an agenda and two documents attached, asking people to review these before the meeting. Your intention was to make sure people were informed about a big decision on bonuses so you could vote as a team. When the meeting begins, you ask the group, "Did you

TABLE 6.2. The bid to avoid responsibility and the reality behind statements with the responsibility switch turned off

Statement	Bid to avoid responsibility	The compassionate truth
"That really made me upset."	By blaming you for my anger, I can avoid expressing it in a healthy way. I can also avoid having a difficult conversation with you about your behavior.	My anger was not caused by you and belongs only to me. It is my responsibility to own my anger and have a conversation with you about your behavior.

(continued)

Statement	Bid to avoid responsibility	The compassionate truth
"You disrespected me."	By isolating responsibility on you for my worth as a human being, I can mask my feelings of embarrassment and defensiveness and try to make them your problem.	Nobody has the power to determine another person's value as a human being. It is my responsibility to express my feelings, advocate for my value, and ask for what I want from you instead.
"It's not my fault that I didn't have the instructions in advance."	By blaming the other person, I avoid dealing with the real issues: how I feel right now and the fact that I am not prepared.	I can't control what others do or don't do, but I can control what I do next. I am 100 percent responsible for how I handle the dilemma I find myself in.
"I expected more from you, you let me down."	By blaming you for not fulfilling an unspoken desire of mine, I get to avoid the transparency and vulnerability that comes with being honest and open about my wishes and the difficult work of seeking a commitment.	I am 100 percent responsible for knowing, sharing, and asking for what I want. Expectations, as they say, are the surest path to disappointment.
"If you do that again, I'll have no choice but to fire you."	By blaming you for my decision to fire you, I can confuse your behavior with my duties as a leader, as if I don't have a choice.	They are responsible for following the standards required to be employed. I am responsible for clarifying and enforcing those standards.

all have a chance to review the documents I sent out?" Several people look at you with blank stares. One person says, "I never got it."

What do you do next? What thoughts go through your head? What feelings do you experience? With the responsibility switch off, you might respond by quickly checking your Sent email folder hoping to prove to yourself that you did your part and that they are at fault. Another way to isolate responsibility would be to poll the group to see who got the email and read it, thereby singling out the people who didn't.

Or you could do what so many well-intentioned leaders do when things don't go as planned: divert attention away from the real issue by saying, "Well, I sent it out last week," as if reminding people that you did your part somehow fixes things. But it doesn't because you aren't dealing with two important issues. The first issue is that you didn't get what you wanted. Several people aren't prepared for your meeting, and that's a problem. The second issue is how you feel about it. Are you angry? Discouraged? Frustrated? Defensive? A leader with their responsibility switch on says to themself, "I can't control what happens to me, but I can control what I do next. How will I take personal responsibility for my feelings and what I want and then address the relevant behaviors in a respectful way?"

What are some better ways to respond with the responsibility switch on? At the end of this next section, you will see examples of responding to a specific conflict challenge without taking on too much or too little responsibility.

Taking Over Responsibility for Others' Feelings, Thoughts, or Behaviors

With the responsibility switch off, taking on too much responsibility for others is easy to do. In that same scenario with the email that several people didn't read, you might assume you are at fault, questioning whether you even sent it to them. If your immediate response is "I'm sorry, I should have checked to see if you all got it first," your responsibility switch is probably off. If you delay the meeting to resend everyone the document while everyone waits, you've taken on too much responsibility for their behaviors.

Table 6.3 includes some more common statements people make and how they show an effort to take on too much responsibility.

Let's revisit the scenario where several members of your executive team aren't prepared for the vote on bonuses. How should a leader respond? Here are two ways you could respond with your responsibility switch on that take on neither too little nor too much responsibility:

- "I feel stressed about this situation because I wanted everyone to be prepared. What ideas do you have for how we can be most productive under these circumstances? It's critical that everyone is up to speed before we vote."
- "I feel discouraged about this. I was looking forward to getting closure on this topic, but we can't vote until everyone is up to speed. This will delay our bonuses. If we postpone until next week and I make sure everyone has it, will you all commit to reviewing the materials in advance so we can come ready to vote?"

In each case, the leader owns their feelings, takes responsibility for what they want, and asks for help to find a solution. In the second response, the leader takes responsibility for enforcing a natural consequence without pointing fingers by focusing on the desired goal rather than acting out a whodunit.

In chapter 4, "The Value Switch," we learned how important vulnerability is and how hard it can be to own and share our emotions

TABLE 6.3. Statements that take on responsibility for feelings and the compassionate truth

Statement	Bid to take over responsibility	The compassionate truth
"I'm sorry I made you mad."	By blaming yourself for the other person's feelings, you don't allow them to own their own emotions, nor do you express your own feelings about what you did.	You are responsible for your behaviors that caused harm and for how you feel about it.
"What she was trying to say is . . ."	By speaking for someone else, you take over the responsibility for their thoughts, make yourself the focus of attention and deprive them of that opportunity and responsibility.	Others are responsible for their thoughts. It's okay to ask questions and encourage them but not speak for them.
"It's probably my fault that I didn't have the instructions in advance."	Defaulting to self-blame for situations you don't yet understand is irresponsible. Pointing the finger at yourself bypasses necessary conflict and real conversations about behaviors.	The real questions are (1) What can we do now under these conditions? and (2) How can we prevent this from happening in the future?
"I'll cover for you this time."	By covering for someone, you are knowingly helping them avoid responsibility and avoiding a necessary boundary or accountability conversation.	Conflict is a necessary part of compassion and can be navigated in a healthy way.

and experiences. Leaders often try to shift responsibility in these situations in an effort to avoid the vulnerability, bypass the conflict, or hide their lack of skill in handling a situation effectively. The first act of personal responsibility as a leader is to get crystal clear about what they are and aren't responsible for. Taking too much or too little responsibility for our own and others' feelings, thoughts, and behaviors has the long-term impact of undermining value and capability. An important leadership skill is helping others navigate this difficult boundary as well.

Attacking or Blaming to Isolate Responsibility

One of the most obvious signs that our responsibility switch is off is calling someone out and publicly shaming them. Here are some examples:

- "What were you thinking!"
- "It's your fault we missed the deadline."
- "You need to step up."
- "Your department is slacking."

These statements, while containing a modicum of truth, are intended to humiliate another person in front of those whose respect and acceptance they desire the most. Isolating responsibility in this way is reckless and abusive and creates an unsafe, toxic work environment.

Behind most attacking and blaming behavior is a leader who feels embarrassed, angry, frustrated, or otherwise desperate. Something has happened that could reflect poorly on them or that they take personally. Not having better tools to deal with it, they lash out, using fear and intimidation to get what they want.

This is not to say that leaders should look the other way or let bad behavior slide. What it means is that they clarify who's responsible for what and have respectful and difficult conversations when needed; no excuses, no blaming, no avoiding.

Turning Conflict into a Win-or-Lose Power Struggle

When our responsibility switch is off, we view conflict as an adversarial situation. Differences and disagreements are viewed as threats to our identity, power, or position, so we enter into conflict expecting a winner and loser. Stephen Karpman's Drama Triangle demonstrates three behavioral roles people play in conflict that distort responsibility. I provide a detailed overview of the three roles and their dynamics in my book *Conflict without Casualties*.[1] Here's a brief overview of the Drama Triangle:

> *Victim*—In conflict, victims take the position of "I'm not okay, you are okay," and assume they are the problem. They compromise their own needs, feelings, and boundaries to keep the peace. They would rather lose the fight than assertively express their feelings.

> *Persecutor*—In conflict, persecutors take the position of "I'm okay, you are not okay." They assume they are right and others are wrong, and they go on the attack to prove their point. They justify their abusive behavior with the excuse that others deserve it.

> *Rescuer*—In conflict, rescuers take the position of "I'm okay, and you would be okay if you let me fix you." They swoop in with unsolicited advice as if others can't think for themselves. They are solutions looking for a problem.

Persecutors recruit victims so they can win. Victims recruit persecutors so they can lose. Victims also recruit rescuers so they can feel broken and helpless. Rescuers recruit victims to feel powerful and boost their egos. In every case, the interactions between these roles in drama lead to either a winner or loser. Energy is spent to feel justified rather than take personal responsibility for feelings, thoughts, and behaviors.

Focusing on Self-Preservation and Self-Promotion

It makes sense that if we work in an environment where responsibility is being isolated, we would want to avoid the bad and cut in front of the line for the good. When our responsibility switch is off and it looks like things aren't going well, we run for cover.

Consider the dilemma in most healthcare settings when a medical provider makes a mistake. As soon as the error is recognized, the first step is to avoid talking, admit nothing, and call the lawyer. Run for cover. Never mind the fear, anxiety, and anguish that might be present in both the provider and patient. At a time when the most compassionate step is to be transparent and focus on the relationship, we are trained to focus on self-preservation instead.

When I fly, I often try to find seats with a little more legroom. I'm six feet four inches tall, so I will often pay a little extra for an exit row because they tend to have more legroom. I did this for a recent flight from Chicago to Orlando, hoping to get some work done on the flight. When I got to my seat, I noticed that it was as cramped as can be, the same or worse than the already tight basic economy seats. What was weird was that this plane had three consecutive exit rows. The ones behind me and in front of me had ample legroom, but mine didn't. I was confused since I had paid extra for this seat.

After completing the verbal consent required by travelers sitting in an exit row, I decided to ask the flight attendant about it, and her response showed me that her responsibility switch was off. "Oh, I'm so sorry. I can't do anything about it, but I'll text the gate agent. Maybe they can help, but this is a full flight. You can ask for a refund from

United if you want." I thanked her for this and set about finding out how to get a refund using my United mobile app.

Unfortunately, it got worse. We couldn't depart due to a faulty air-flow system that was connected somehow to starting the engine. After an hour of waiting while the plane got hotter and hotter and I became more claustrophobic, we were invited to deplane since they had no idea how long it would take to solve the problem.

After I deplaned, I took the opportunity to speak with the gate agent about my cramped exit row seat. When I explained my situation to the gate agent and asked about options, she looked at my boarding pass and told me, "This isn't an exit row." I was flummoxed since my boarding pass said "exit row" on it, my seat was next to a door that had EXIT printed on it, and I had been forced to give a verbal yes to the flight attendant that I would perform the duties necessary in the event of an emergency.

I shared this with the gate agent, who wasn't phased. She again told me this wasn't an exit row. When I persisted, she changed her tune, now telling me that my seat was in an exit row, but it did not have extra legroom. Finally, we were on the same page. I then asked her why they would charge extra for a seat without extra legroom. "Because you are closer to economy plus, and those seats are extra." This is when I decided to take my concern elsewhere because this gate agent didn't seem interested in being helpful.

Instead of taking time to understand my situation or even show some empathy for my confusion, she discounted my reality and made excuses. Perhaps she was in self-preservation mode considering the circumstances.

Four days later, when checking in for my flight back to Chicago, I did a little sleuthing. I found out that this particular exit row on this particular aircraft has less legroom. And when selecting the seat, the fine print indicates as much. Knowing this, I felt a little better: at least I hadn't been duped by the airline when selecting my seat. But I wondered how the gate agent might have responded to me with her responsibility switch on. If I were coaching this agent, or perhaps the entire service crew of United Airlines, I would suggest something like this:

> Sir, I can imagine it was disappointing and confusing for you to pay extra for a seat, expecting more legroom, only to find out that this row doesn't have it. And to make matters worse, you've been sitting in that seat for an hour on the tarmac while we figure out this air handling problem. I am so sorry about that. When it comes to exit rows, this plane is unique because that one row doesn't have extra legroom. I'm not sure why they charged you more, but I would be happy to explore this further with you once we figure out the next steps for getting everyone on another plane. Meanwhile, if you'd like to ask for a refund, I can show you how to do that on the app. How does that sound?

How much energy is spent in most workplaces maneuvering to stay out of harm's way, shift blame in case something backfires, make excuses, or otherwise play it safe? These reactions are a consequence of having the responsibility switch off.

What about when things go well? Then everyone is clamoring to be in the spotlight. But because responsibility is isolated, there's never enough credit to go around, so people make it a competition for who thought of a solution first or who did the most work. Someone wins, and the others lose.

When our responsibility switch is off, our behaviors promote an inconsistent environment where people can't count on each other, don't trust each other, and worry more about looking out for themselves than helping others.

Turn On Your Responsibility Switch

Because people are responsible, everyone is accountable for their feelings, thoughts, and actions.

Here are five clusters of behavioral strategies that help leaders turn on, and keep on, their responsibility switch:

- Take ownership of your emotions, thoughts, and behaviors.
- Allow others to take ownership of their emotions, thoughts, and behaviors.
- Ask directly and assertively for what you want and need.
- Enforce boundaries, standards, and commitments without blaming, attacking, or threatening.
- Keep the most important thing the most important thing.

Take Ownership of Your Emotions, Thoughts, and Behaviors

Scott Shute, who was the head of Mindfulness and Compassion Programs at LinkedIn, has dedicated his professional career to understanding happiness and helping others achieve happiness. He believes that happiness is based not on what happens to us but how we choose to respond.[2] Responding with our responsibility switch on starts with simply observing our internal experiences without judgment. Seeing and accepting them for what they are allows us to be present and intentional with how we respond. This step is especially important when we experience conflict, when unexpected events happen, or when life seems out of our control.

Emotions are a product of how we interpret and give meaning to our affective experiences. Owning our emotions means taking the time to understand why we feel a certain way and how we are interpreting what's going on around and inside us. This step isn't about what others said or did but how we uniquely interact with what happens.

Two people can have different emotional responses to the same stimulus. This proves the existence of an individual component, a part for which each of us is responsible. Leaders often miss or don't pay attention to a host of details that influence their emotional responses to situations, such as past experiences, belief systems, their need to be perceived a certain way by others, and personality. Taking responsibility for our emotions and thoughts means understanding these influences, coming to grips with their impact, reconciling past issues if needed, and fully embracing that all of these are part of who we are. Only then can we choose our behaviors with awareness and intention.

Without doing this inside work, leaders find themselves responding reflexively to situations, often without awareness, repeating unhelpful habits.

Disclosing and explaining our feelings to others is an important way to take responsibility. Here are some examples:

- "I'm feeling anxious about this rollout because I want it to reflect positively on our department."
- "I overreacted to your comment because it reminded me of a past situation where I didn't feel respected. That's on me, not you."
- "I'm discouraged that some of you aren't prepared because I put a lot into planning this meeting and was looking forward to our discussion of the strategy."

Apologizing is another way to take responsibility for your emotions, thoughts, and behaviors. When we've let someone down or made a mistake that impacted others, a sincere apology is important.

Making an apology with our responsibility switch off will usually fail because it isn't sincere and doesn't address the real issue.

I get a kick out of apologies made with the responsibility switch off. Here are a few that are particularly common and comical:

- "I'm sorry if you were offended by something I said."
- "I'm sorry for whatever I did that bothered you."
- "Okay, fine! I'm sorry."
- "I'm sorry. Are you happy now?"
- "I didn't mean to, but if it makes you feel better, I'm sorry."

Here are some examples of good apologies with the responsibility switch on:

- "I feel embarrassed about what I said in the meeting. That comment was inappropriate and disrespectful. I am really sorry. I will watch my words more closely in the future."
- "I am angry at myself for missing the meeting. By not being there, I held up our progress on a critical component of the strategic plan. I am sorry. What can I do to make it up to the team?"

These two examples demonstrate that the person is aware of their feelings, understands their specific damaging behavior, and is seeking to make amends. They are taking responsibility for only their own emotions, thoughts, and behaviors. Nothing more, nothing less.

If happiness is not about what happens to us but how we respond, then forgiveness is the ultimate act of personal responsibility. I came to appreciate this through my conversation with Randy Conley.[3] Randy is vice president and trust practice leader for the Ken Blanchard Companies. He is coauthor, with Ken Blanchard, of the book *Simple Truths of Leadership: 52 Ways to Be a Servant Leader and Build Trust.*[4]

Simple truth #52 in Randy and Ken's book says, "*Forgiveness is letting go of all hope for a better past.*"

When I read this the first time, I got a lump in my throat. That's a tough reality to swallow, and on the surface this seems kind of depressing. I asked Randy to help me with this. He explained that we often hold on to unforgiveness because we think it's hurting the other person. We're sticking it to them. The reality is, though, while we are harboring resentment, that other person is probably off living their best life. Forgiving others isn't about letting them off the hook but instead taking responsibility for our own happiness. It's how we take care of ourselves, stay healthy, keep our tank full, and show up with compassion.

Leaders who aren't able to forgive others, including themselves, are living in the past and stealing energy from the present.

Allow Others to Take Ownership of Their Emotions, Thoughts, and Behaviors

Taking ownership of our own emotions, thoughts, and behaviors doesn't mean we don't care about what others feel, think, and do. It simply means we don't take it on as our own. This changes how a leader responds to others around issues of accountability.

As a leader, you probably receive many invitations every day to take on responsibility for others' issues. Employees complain about what their coworkers are doing and want you to fix it. Your boss asks you to do something that encroaches on a personal boundary. Your children act like money grows on trees in the backyard. These situations are difficult because they are never simple and usually involve strong emotions or a sense of urgency.

Keeping our responsibility switch on in these types of situations involves three important steps: validating the other person's experience without taking it on, inviting them to be part of the solution, and clarifying boundaries. It might sound like one of these responses:

- "I'm sorry about the conflict you are having with your coworker. What support do you want to be able to address this directly with her? I am willing to support you having that conversation, but I won't do it for you."
- "I know how important this is for you. Is there someone else who could join you tonight? We agreed that I can attend my son's soccer games on Wednesday nights, and that's tonight."
- "That sounds tough. I hate it when I can't afford something I want. What else can you do this weekend? I am not going to advance your allowance."

When people make excuses or don't seem to want to take responsibility for their emotions, thoughts, and behaviors, it might be an issue of willingness. Marlene Chism is an expert in change and conflict. She works with leaders who are facing resistance around behavior change. She believes that nothing happens without willingness. If you don't understand this as a leader, you might let your responsibility switch turn off. When people appear resistant, either taking over the responsibility or getting into negative power struggles with them around it feels easier. Instead, Marlene recommends zoning in on willingness.

Let's say an employee makes the excuse "I can't get my paperwork done on time because the computer system is too complicated." Consider this response that focuses on willingness: "It is complicated. If we could help you learn to use the system more efficiently, would you be willing to get your paperwork done on time?"

A salesperson complains that they can't meet their quota because of economic conditions, even though their peers are meeting the quota. You could focus on willingness with this response: "It is difficult in these tough times. If you could get insights and tips from your peers, would you be willing to apply them to meet your quota?"

A child complains they need new shoes and wants an advance on their allowance. Instead of preaching to the child about saving money or complaining that they can't afford it, imagine this response: "You are right, new shoes sure are expensive. If you had a way to earn extra money, would you be willing to do it?"

The approach, outlined with much more detail in Marlene's book *From Conflict to Courage: How to Stop Avoiding and Start Leading*, helps leaders keep responsibility where it lies.[5] An employee is responsible for meeting performance expectations. The leader is responsible for supporting them, making resources available, and clarifying and reinforcing the boundaries.

Ask Directly and Assertively for What You Want and Need

Advocating for yourself is a compassionate act. Ask for what you want and need to be safe, healthy, productive, and happy.

What kind of work environment helps you be your best? Have you asked for support in achieving that?

What type of feedback is most helpful for you to do your best work? Have you told this to your team and asked for it?

What charges your battery? Have you shared this with your boss and asked for them to notice what matters most to you?

In our work with leaders, we focus heavily on self-awareness and advocacy around what helps us do our best. So many leaders are focused on everyone else that they don't pay attention to what makes them tick. The notion of asking for what they want and need to be more safe, healthy, productive, and happy seems selfish. Or they fear that nobody will care. Contrary to their fears, when teams begin sharing these truths with each other, it unlocks new levels of trust, energy, and connection. Nobody wants to waste energy interacting in ways that aren't helpful. Most people are hungry for guidance on how to help each other succeed. To quote Jerry Maguire's iconic line from the movie of the same name, "Help me help you!"

I believe that this idea should be central to the conversation in every performance evaluation process. Every supervisor-employee relationship should include intentional conversations about what they each need to be safe, healthy, productive, and happy, along with action plans outlining behavioral commitments to support those needs. When these conversations become part of a team process, the team starts to thrive.

Enforce Boundaries, Standards, and Commitments without Blaming, Attacking, or Threatening

Previously I mentioned Laura Cole, who works with leaders and teams around organizational culture development and change management. Laura's most powerful tool is Watson, who has an uncanny ability to detect and reflect the kind of energy people are sending out. Watson is an integral part of Laura's leadership development programs. When I spoke with Laura about compassion, she talked about the importance of boundaries and how so many leaders struggle with this.[6] Watson has a habit of nibbling shirts. Yet successful executives at the top of their game regularly allow him to bite holes in their shirts because they don't enforce boundaries.

Watson is a horse. Why do successful executives allow a horse to bite holes in their shirts? Laura explained that most leaders make the excuse that they don't want to be mean or don't know how to stop it. Being unclear or inconsistent on boundaries isn't kind or helpful. As Laura noted, it deprives others of a more healthy way to interact with us and form a meaningful relationship. Boundaries are a foundation for strong relationships. Furthermore, when we don't set and enforce boundaries, we can easily slip into forming negative opinions of others who seem to disrespect our wants and needs.

I can personally attest to the power of working with horses around personal and team dynamics. If you haven't had the opportunity to do so, I highly recommend it.

Enforcing boundaries, standards, and commitments isn't easy, and you don't have to be mean about it. But it does require clarity about your role as a leader and the courage to speak clearly and consistently. It also requires that leaders let go of trying to manage other people's emotions and reactions. Here are some examples of healthy boundary setting without attacking, blaming, or threatening:

- "These are the standards we have set, and it's not negotiable that you meet them to be employed here."
- "We agreed I could attend my daughter's volleyball game tonight, so I will not stay late and work on the project."
- "I won't cover for you because it's your responsibility to come up with your own ideas on this project."
- "You have been late three times this month, so I am initiating a corrective action plan."
- "Please include me next time on the meeting invite. It's important that I am involved in this decision."

For leaders who favor the value and capability switches over the responsibility switch, setting and enforcing boundaries can be a challenge. They may convince themselves that if they are just kind and supportive, others will somehow step up and take ownership of their behavior. They won't. That's because every day, in every interaction, leaders are training others how to treat them.

Keep the Most Important Thing the Most Important Thing

Sticking to your priorities is one of my favorite bits of advice for leaders. At least once a day, I hear this phrase in my head, especially when I find myself down in the weeds, thinking I need to have all the answers. Living out this principle involves two critical practices: identifying what the most important thing is and then maintaining focus on it. Responsibility hinges on discerning and communicating what's most important.

One of my partners, Rob Wert, is famous on our team for reminding us about "first principles." When we get off on tangents or down a rabbit trail, Rob asks us to elevate our conversation back to what matters most. What fundamental principles and values are at stake? What are we ultimately trying to achieve? This helps us refocus from the particulars to the big picture. This reminder is especially helpful when we get too attached to one approach or perspective or distracted by details that aren't helpful.

Leaders can easily get attached to a particular outcome, idea, or solution that they believe will solve the problem and serve the goal. Once they do this, however, they stop listening. They stop exploring possibilities. This means that their teams aren't empowered to get creative and take ownership. Have you ever been asked for input only to learn later that your leader already had their mind made up? What a waste.

One way for leaders to escape this trap is to elevate their perspective from solutions to principles. Instead of focusing on solutions, focus on the values, principles, and goals that need to be met. Explain these to your team, then ask them to come up with solutions. Instead of focusing on finding solutions, you can evaluate if and how their solutions can serve those first principles.

The Barrett Values Centre has a saying: *"Values unite, beliefs divide."*[7] Tom Henry, director of consulting, invites leaders to avoid focusing on the individual beliefs and conclusions we hold and instead focus on the higher order values that bring us together. Tom explains that focusing on beliefs is about *I*, while focusing on values is about *we*.[8] When our attachment is not to being right but to being whole and aligned, then we can move away from our ego-centered solutions into a dialogue about what serves our values and higher purpose.

Together, these five clusters of behaviors turn on and keep on the responsibility switch to promote an environment of consistency, dignity, respect, ownership, and accountability.

Main Points

The main points of this chapter are summarized in table 6.4.

Turn your responsibility switch on with these behaviors:

- Take ownership of your emotions, thoughts, and behaviors.
- Allow others to take ownership of their emotions, thoughts, and behaviors.
- Ask directly and assertively for what you want and need.
- Enforce boundaries, standards, and commitments without blaming, attacking or threatening.
- Keep the most important thing the most important thing.

TABLE 6.4. Summary of the differences when a responsibility switch is off versus on

Responsibility switch is off	Responsibility switch is on
Avoid responsibility for our emotions, thoughts, and behaviors. Take on too much responsibility for others' emotions, thoughts, or behaviors.	Take personal responsibility for our emotions, thoughts, and behaviors—no more, no less.
Use fear, intimidation, or shame to influence behaviors.	Use healthy, assertive communication around boundaries and commitments.
Approach conflicts as win-or-lose adversarial situations.	Engage in positive conflicts that create connection, trust, and ownership.
Focus on self-preservation and self-promotion.	Keep focus on values and principles that unite people around a common purpose.

Quiz Answers

Table 6.5 shows the answers to the responsibility switch interaction quiz in table 6.1.

Commentary on Quiz Answers

Let's explore the responsibility switch interaction quiz answers from table 6.5 in more depth.

1. A real apology with the responsibility switch on includes owning your behavior and working toward a solution. I believe that good apologies are a lost art. We don't teach people how to do it, and we rarely model what a good apology looks like. I offer

TABLE 6.5. Answers to the responsibility switch interaction quiz

What you observe	Is the responsibility switch on? Y/N
1. When you make a mistake, you own it, apologize, and make it right.	Y
2. Your coworker says, "The way you talked to that customer made everyone so embarrassed."	N
3. You tell your work partner, "We agreed to complete the list by the weekend. You can count on me to do my part."	Y
4. Your boss seems to have high expectations because you're always coming up short, but you don't have direct conversations about what they are.	N
5. After your friend makes a critical mistake, you say, "What can you do differently so this doesn't happen again?"	Y
6. Personal gain takes priority over team or company goals.	N
7. You make a mistake, and your coworker says, "You made your bed, now you have to lie in it."	N
8. Your coworker says to you, "I feel embarrassed. It's not okay to talk to customers like that."	Y

a template for making great apologies in my blog post "How to Make a Better Apology" on the Next Element website.[9] You can use it for yourself or when coaching and mentoring others.

2. The problem isn't that your coworker confronted you. The problem is that they blamed you for other people's embarrassment. Nobody is responsible for another person's feelings.

They are responsible for their behaviors, though, which probably should be addressed.

If your coworker's responsibility switch were on, they might have said, "I felt so embarrassed when you blamed the customer because it was our mistake. We should always take time to explore the situation and ask questions before forming conclusions about what happened."

3. By telling your work partner they can count on you, you've set the tone for shared responsibility on the project.

4. Few things are more frustrating than a boss who is impossible to please. Having high standards is great, but it's critical to communicate these to your employees clearly and consistently. Withholding information to keep people guessing is not compassionate. Situations like this won't change until you change your approach.

   His responsibility switch might be off now, but you can invite your boss to turn it on by turning your switch on. Imagine talking to your boss and saying, "I'm struggling with something, and I want your help. I respect your high standards and want to work toward them. Yet I often don't know what you want. I'm committed to checking in with you more regularly. Would you be willing to share with me what you are looking for so we are clear about goals?"

5. A mistake is an opportunity to learn and grow. As a friend, you can help that process along by inviting your friend to make changes in behavior going forward. Your comment focuses on the behavior, not the person. Apologies are a start, but after a failure of any kind it's important to make new commitments for the future.

6. Although it may seem obvious that prioritizing personal agendas over collective goals isn't helpful for the team, this behavior is all too common in our world today. Politicians pursue fame, money, and notoriety over doing what's best for their

constituency or community. Leaders pursue personal power agendas instead of what's best for the team. Imagine a world where responsibility meant more than just looking out for your own self-interests.

7. Responding with "You made your bed, now you have to lie in it" is a great example of how not to respond when someone messes up. Your coworker might feel justified with their sarcastic comment, but they've left you to struggle alone. That's not compassion. See number 5 for a better response.

8. Responding like this is much preferable to prompt number 2. In this situation, your coworker owns their own feelings and confronts the behavior of the other person without attacking their character or integrity.

PART III

IMPLEMENTATION

Build Your Culture of Compassionate Accountability

CHAPTER 7

HOW TO BUILD YOUR CULTURE OF COMPASSIONATE ACCOUNTABILITY

ANYONE CAN challenge their own myths about compassion, turn on their compassion mindset switches, and embrace the potential of Compassionate Accountability. This chapter is for teams and organizations looking to embed these concepts into their culture. Additional resources are available by visiting CompassionateAccountabilityBook .com.

Are you ready to build your culture of Compassionate Accountability?

To get started, figures 7.1 and 7.2 offer a quick summary of the three switches of the compassion mindset. Use them to review the consequences to work culture when the switches are off versus on.

When the switches are off, the consequences for work culture can include the following:

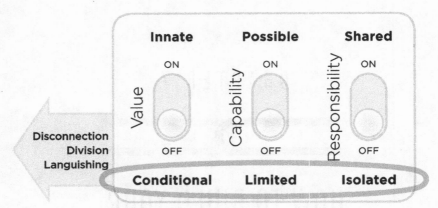

FIGURE 7.1. When the switches are off.
Designed by Scott Light, CG Studios.

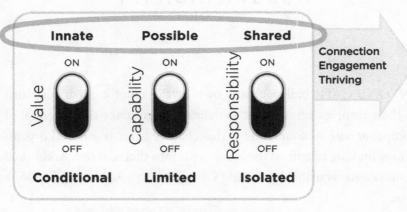

FIGURE 7.2. When the switches are on.
Designed by Scott Light, CG Studios.

- Lack of confidence
- Underutilized talent
- Fear and negativity
- Discrimination
- Dependence
- Resentment
- Morale problems
- Retention problems
- Burnout

When the switches are on, the benefits for work culture can include the following:

- Confidence
- Application of everyone's skills
- Buy-in, ownership, and engagement
- Positivity and innovation
- Collaboration
- Productivity
- Inclusion

Necessary but Not Sufficient

All three compassion mindset switches are necessary but not sufficient on their own for Compassionate Accountability to manifest in your culture, especially if your goal is to engage and retain current and future generations of employees. All three must be on for energy to flow and for Compassionate Accountability to be fully realized. Each switch paves the way and supports the others. Here are the typical cultural consequences of having one of the switches turned off while the other two are on.

When the value switch is off, teams and organizations engage in problem-solving and follow through, but people don't feel safe. They worry about making mistakes and comply out of fear rather than connection and engagement.

When the capability switch is off, cultures often will have a family-like atmosphere, demonstrate loyalty to the organization's mission and leadership, but lack innovation. They struggle to adapt and stay relevant.

When the responsibility switch is off, organizations suffer from a lack of consistency, integrity, and follow-through. They are more likely to fail during hard times because they don't have a strong foundation.

The Future of Leadership

Research on employee engagement and retention revealed that millennials and Gen Zers have different wants and needs. One of the best summaries of this literature that I have seen is contained in Mark C. Crowley's book, *Lead from the Heart*.[1] Mark outlines five major trends that drive engagement for the new generation of employees:

- They want to know their work has purpose.
- They don't want a boss, they want a coach.
- They want much more frequent feedback.
- They want to focus on their strengths.
- They want investment in their growth and development.

Mark distills the current research into table 7.1, outlining how a leader's focus has to change from the past to lead in the future. I've added a column connecting each of the three switches of the compassion mindset—value, capability, and responsibility—to Mark's categories of leadership focus. You might see even more connections than I did. Notice how these future-facing leadership changes involve all three switches of the compassion mindset in equal measure.

TABLE 7.1. The change in leadership, past to future, aligned with the compassion mindset. Used with permission of Mark C. Crowley.

Past	Future	Compassion mindset switch
My paycheck	My purpose	Value, responsibility
My satisfaction	My development	Capability, responsibility
My boss	My coach	Value, capability
My annual review	My ongoing conversations	Capability, responsibility
My weaknesses	My strengths	Value, capability
My job	My life	Value

VCR

Some readers might recognize the acronym VCR to mean *video cassette recorder*. Our clients have repurposed it to mean *value, capability,* and *responsibility*. This acronym is a handy way to remind ourselves of the three switches. Are your switches on? Is your VCR turned on?

Change Starts with Me

Keeping our switches on means we recognize that we have control over only our own behaviors. This means we focus first on turning on and keeping on our own switches. Any efforts leaders make to influence other people's behaviors and the culture must come from a place of having our own switches on first.

The Compassionate Accountability Assessment

Before you go any further, let's do a thorough self-assessment of Compassionate Accountability in your life. Consult the appendix for a template that will help you to assess Compassionate Accountability in yourself, your team, and your organization. When you are finished, use the results to continue reflecting, discussing, and setting goals. You can also download a digital copy of the Compassionate Accountability Assessment by visiting CompassionateAccountabilityBook.com.

Here are some prompts to consider as you reflect on your results, share with others, process as a team, or set goals:

- Where are your strength zones? How do these help build a thriving culture? List the benefits.
- Where are your danger zones? How are these contributing to a toxic culture? What is it costing you? List the consequences.
- Where are your opportunity zones? How can you build on these to create strengths? Describe where you could focus next.
- Explore consistency and balance within each domain (e.g., "myself"). If any of the switches is more than one point apart from the others, this represents an imbalance. The first section of this chapter described typical cultural consequences when one switch is turned off relative to the others. How does this fit with your experience?
- Explore consistency across domains for a given switch. For example, what are the value scores for you, your team, and your organization? How do you explain the differences? How do the differences impact you, your team, and your organization?
- What goals would you like to set? How will you achieve these goals? For suggestions on where to start, see the section later in this chapter called "Embedding Compassionate Accountability: Where to Start."

Here are some suggested action steps based on how you scored on the Compassionate Accountability Assessment. Use these as general guidelines on where to start:

0–1 = *Danger zone*—Chances are you are experiencing significant negative consequences in your culture and organization due to lack of Compassionate Accountability. Low engagement, high turnover, low customer satisfaction, and gross inefficiencies are making it difficult to meet your goals. The problem isn't "out there." It's your culture.

Stop the bus, evaluate what's going on, and make changes immediately. Get help now.

1–2 = *Potential zone*—Compassionate Accountability is trying to break forth. Your organization likely has pockets of compassion. This might include individuals who are taking matters into their own hands, going against the grain. It could involve leaders, teams or departments that are stepping up and doing the right thing, even though these acts are countercultural. The best thing to do is nurture present potential.

Learn from compassion champions, support them, nurture what they are doing, and use it as a catalyst for change. Start measuring the impact of their efforts and share it with your organization. Invite them to teach others what they are doing. Set benchmarks and goals for increasing the presence of the desired behaviors.

2–2.5 = *Opportunity zone*—You are making progress. Compassionate Accountability is taking hold, becoming more accepted and normalized in the culture. Momentum is building, and opportunity is great. Take a moment to reflect on how far you've come, and celebrate it.

Solidify Compassionate Accountability in your culture so it becomes part of your DNA. Embed it into the systems and processes that keep your organization running. Celebrate successes, and share the metrics to back it up. If any naysayers or saboteurs remain, especially among top leadership, now is the time to send the clear message, "Get on board or get out." You won't get to the next level unless you have a strong, aligned group of leaders who are walking the talk and holding each other accountable.

2.5–3 = *Strength zone*—Compassionate Accountability is alive and active. Momentum is strong. You are probably enjoying the benefits in terms of higher engagement, lower turnover, and higher customer satisfaction. Business success follows from that. Congratulations!

Now is the time to remember that the biggest threat to future success is past success. Don't get complacent. Keep setting goals that stretch you to become better. Aspire to be the employer of choice, the leader in your industry, the best place to work.

Setting Behavior Norms

Behavior norms represent a group's commitment to particular behaviors. It's like saying to each other and your organization, "You can count on these behaviors from us."

Each switch includes specific clusters of observable behaviors. Each one plays an important role in turning on and keeping on the other switches. Here is a process for establishing behavior norms for the three switches:

1. *Prepare*—Invite each member of the group to read and study chapters 4–6 in this book so they are familiar with the behaviors for each switch.
2. *Reflect*—Invite each member of the group to complete the Compassionate Accountability Assessment in the appendix, rating themselves, their team, and the organization.
3. *Share*—Meet with group members to share and compare ratings. Discuss any insights. There are no right or wrong

ratings. What's most important is to foster a safe and curious space to explore what people are feeling and thinking about the switches. Consolidating and aggregating team member ratings can provide a baseline if desired.

4. *Assess the current state*—As a team, work together to create a list of current behaviors that indicate the switches are on or off. To keep the value and responsibility switches on, adhere to this rule: you can list only your own behaviors. Calling out others is not allowed. Be as specific as possible about behaviors.

5. *Develop norms*—As a team, work together to create a list of desired behaviors that will indicate the switches are on. Be as specific as possible. Use chapters 4–6 and the items in the Compassionate Accountability Assessment as your guide. I usually advise teams to identify two to three behaviors for each switch, ones that will make the biggest positive impact. Keep it simple, focused, and realistic.

6. *Commit to norms*—Each person on the team must commit to the behavior norms before moving to the next step. Committing is more than a vote. Committing is informed consent coupled with a public declaration of intent. Each person should indicate their understanding of the behavior and declare their intent to adhere to this behavior going forward. Until every person is ready to do this, more discussion and refinement of the norms (step 5) is needed. Don't rush this step.

7. *Anticipate failure*—Aspirational goals are wonderful, but they don't mean much until they are challenged. Once you've finalized your list of behavior norms, anticipate and prepare for what happens when people don't follow through. Have a candid group discussion of when and how people are most likely to fail. Where will it be most challenging to implement new behaviors, and why?

8. *Prepare for accountability conversations*—When people fail, and they will, how will you address it? This is where your team develops an accountability plan for helping each other get back on track. Having a plan for how you will talk to each other to get back on track helps build confidence. If your team doesn't have good conflict skills, it might be worth investing in some training because these conversations will be difficult and emotionally charged.

9. *Make a public commitment*—Now you are ready to share your behavior norms with the wider community. Create a communication plan to share your norms with your organization. Publicly declaring your intentions is an important accountability step. Following up with actual behaviors is where your resolve is tested. Getting back on track when you fall short is where integrity is established.

10. *Regularly review and reset*—Behavior norms must be a central part of leadership conversations. Make time to regularly review norms, assess adherence and progress, and make necessary adjustments to keep them alive and central to daily interactions.

Some groups can self-facilitate, and some prefer or need a third party to assist the process of establishing behavior norms. There's not a right or wrong way, only what helps your team feel most safe and invited to contribute.

Turning on, and keeping on, our switches is easier said than done. The process of self-reflection and setting behavior norms might reveal skill gaps. Compassionate Accountability is a social and emotional tool kit that requires self-awareness, self-management, and interpersonal communication skills. If you experience resistance to culture change, it might be because of skill deficits among your leaders. If so, invest in getting them the training and coaching they need to consistently exhibit the desired behaviors. Expecting a leader to exhibit new behaviors when they don't know how is unfair.

Embedding Compassionate Accountability: Where to Start

For Compassionate Accountability to become what culture expert and author Seth Godin describes as how "people like us do things like this," requires embedding it into the systems and processes that support your culture.[2] Here are some suggestions on where to start:

Talent acquisition—Recruit and hire for a compassion mindset. Adapt your recruiting and interviewing processes to evaluate for the three switches. Evaluate if candidates have their switches on and how they keep their switches on under stress.

Talent development—Train for the compassion mindset. Evaluate the minimum compassion mindset behavioral competencies you want at each level of the organization. Provide training for those competencies.

Performance evaluation and support—Determine the most basic behavioral expectations for each of the three switches and build these into job descriptions. Measure and evaluate employees on these behaviors.

Discipline—How does your organization handle performance gaps and behavior problems? Evaluate your current processes and policies through the lens of the three switches. Are behavior problems addressed in a way that uplifts value, capability, and responsibility? One of the case studies in the next chapter shows how a hospital replaced progressive discipline with Compassionate Accountability and is experiencing positive results.

Mission, vision, and values—Evaluate your mission, vision, and values to see how well they embody the compassion mindset. Which switches are on? Which ones are off or absent? Where could you update to be more consistent with your behavior norms?

Key performance indicators—The research is clear that compassion improves business outcomes. Now it's time for you to measure it in your organization.

I just finished filling out my customer service survey from that trip on United Airlines I described earlier. As I documented my experience and was asked to share specifics, I realized that it all comes down to Compassionate Accountability. If any one of the switches is off, customer service and customer experience suffers. My survey, and I'm guessing the surveys of dozens more travelers on that same flight, will tell a story of how much Compassionate Accountability was present in those critical moments.

If a culture of Compassionate Accountability is important to you, it's critical that you connect it to your KPIs. What metrics are most important to you? How might these metrics be impacted by bringing more Compassionate Accountability into every interaction? How will you know?

Include These Three Questions in Every Survey

Daily interactions determine the quality of your culture, which determines the strength of your brand. If you want to assess the presence of Compassionate Accountability in your culture, embed a version of the following three questions into every employee, customer, and patient survey you do. Why not make these part of your 360-degree evaluations, performance reviews, and customer focus groups? Why stop there? Build them into your daily huddles, check-ins, and pulse surveys.

- After interactions with my (employee/supervisor/caregiver/ customer service representative), I feel more safe and worthwhile as a person.

  Strongly agree   Agree   Disagree   Strongly disagree

  Describe any behaviors to support your answer _____

  _____

  _____

- After interactions with my (employee/supervisor/caregiver/ customer service representative), I feel more confident and capable.

  Strongly agree   Agree   Disagree   Strongly disagree

  Describe any behaviors to support your answer _____

  _____

  _____

- After interactions with my (supervisor/caregiver/customer service representative), I feel more accountable and empowered.

  Strongly agree   Agree   Disagree   Strongly disagree

  Describe any behaviors to support your answer _____

  _____

  _____

Answers to these questions will be revealing and instructive. Want to take it to the next level? Make the survey anonymous, but give people the opportunity to identify themselves if they want to. Then track the proportion of people who chose to be identified. This is your safety index. It will give you a pretty accurate picture of how safe people feel and how much they trust leadership. If you want to increase your safety index, increase the number of interactions people have with their switches on.

Main Points

- When the switches are off, people will experience disconnection, division, and languishing. When the switches are on, people will experience connection, engagement, and a thriving culture.
- Each of the three switches is necessary but not sufficient on its own to ensure a culture of Compassionate Accountability.
- The main trends driving engagement for the new generation of employees can be addressed with the three switches.
- Change starts with you. You have control over only your own behaviors and choices.
- An honest evaluation of your culture using the Compassionate Accountability Assessment can help you determine whether you are in the danger zone, potential zone, opportunity zone, or strength zone.
- Setting behavior norms is a helpful way for leadership teams to embed Compassionate Accountability into their daily interactions.
- Start embedding compassionate accountability into your culture with these six areas of focus: talent acquisition; talent development; performance evaluation and support; discipline; mission vision and values; and key performance indicators.
- You can begin immediately by surveying your employees, customers, patients, or other stakeholders on where they experience switches in their daily interactions.

CHAPTER 8

CASE STUDIES

REAL-LIFE EXAMPLES are the best illustrations. Here are four examples of organizations that are embedding Compassionate Accountability into their cultures. After each case study, I share some key takeaways that anyone can apply to activate the compassion mindset and bring more Compassionate Accountability to their workplace.

Case Study 1

This case study shows how one regional healthcare system used three switches to update its principles in action. The CEO of a large regional healthcare system recognized the stress and toll that the COVID-19 pandemic was taking on their culture. He had a vision to go from good to great by embedding Compassionate Accountability into their team. He wanted to invest in the resilience of his leaders and bring them together around a common goal for a more compassionate culture. He recognized that change starts from the top and that the key to thriving in an increasingly complex healthcare environment was a strong and resilient leadership culture.

They started with a comprehensive leader-development program that included the executive team, all division directors, all medical directors, and all executive support staff. Focus was on self-awareness and self-management of personality as a leader, essential compassion skills, and positive conflict skills. Along the way, they began looking for ways to bring the concepts of Compassionate Accountability more fully into their daily routines.

One of the first things they looked at was their Principles in Action document. This guiding document outlined the core principles to which they aspired in all interactions as a leadership team. After reviewing their existing document, they decided to update it to reflect their commitment to the three switches. Here's what they came up with:

- Positive and compassionate conflict is healthy and is the foundation that trust is built on.
- Trust creates and sustains effective, efficient, and compassionate leadership teams that drive the culture of the organization.
- We are responsible for the success of the organization. Drama diverts time, energy, and resources away from our goals, strategic priorities, and mission-critical activities. Drama can lead to distress.
- By articulating and expressing our thoughts authentically and managing our responses in appropriate and accountable ways, we have the ability to create positive and productive experiences.

The executive team also covered how they would keep their value, capability, and responsibility switches on. In terms of value, here are their principles in action:

- We value each team member and their unique skills and experiences.
- Communication is key. Transparency belongs at the table.

- Self-awareness and emotional intelligence are valued and help in understanding strengths and weaknesses.
- Authenticity and vulnerability drive trust in a team.
- We value sharing connections and strengthening relationships. That creates a sense of belonging and encourages innovation and recognition of a team.

Here is what they had to say about their capability switch:

- Individually and collectively we are capable.
- It is more important to be effective than right.
- Balancing care, kindness, and concern creates an environment for compassionate conflict. We will take the following actions:
  - Participate in tough conversations.
  - Separate the person from the behavior.
  - Speak honestly with respect and dignity.
  - Take responsibility for emotions without blaming.
  - Own up to behaviors, and ask others to do the same.
  - Deal with issues in a timely way instead of letting them fester.
  - Communicate directly and candidly.
  - Show vulnerability and openness.
  - Struggle with others instead of against them.

Here is what they had to say about their responsibility switch:

- As individuals we are responsible for leadership and outcomes of our respective areas; as a team we are responsible for the success of our organization.
- We are emotionally responsible for our own feelings, actions, and behaviors.
- "Self-fulness," making sure your tank is full before helping others, supports resiliency and keeps us energized to serve others;

we are each responsible for being self-ful. (See chapter 12 for more on this concept.)

- Inclusiveness is the soil in which diversity and equity can take root; we are each responsible for creating a culture of inclusiveness.
- We are responsible for being present in each moment.

For this organization and its leadership team, Principles in Action is a living, breathing document that outlines their aspirations as a culture.

What You Can Do

Here are some ideas of what you can do to activate your compassion mindset:

- Review your mission, vision, and values statements. Do they reflect the compassion mindset? Which switches are on, off, or absent altogether? What changes do you want to make?
- Do you have documents similar to Principles in Action? If not, consider creating one—a public commitment of how leadership will model the principles most important to your organization and its customers.
- Review your code of conduct. Does it reflect the compassion mindset? Why or why not? Do you want to update it?
- Explore how you can be more self-ful as a leadership team. Self-fulness is the practice of taking care of one's own needs to be energized to serve others. (There's more on this concept in chapter 12.)

Case Study 2

This case study shows how one school district created behavior norms for educational leaders. The superintendent of a school district in the midwestern United States had a vision to create a dynamic and thriving school culture by embedding Compassionate Accountability. He saw imbalance among the three switches within school culture and knew that value, capability, and responsibility needed to be embraced in equal measure to take their culture to the next level. In his experience, he had seen that the key to student success was a thriving leadership culture and strong relationships between principals and teachers.

We helped the district map out a two-year leadership culture change process that included assessment and training for all principals and department heads and culture-wide orientation to the principles of Compassionate Accountability.

Once the leaders had been orientated to the principles of Compassionate Accountability and the compassion mindset, they were charged with developing a set of behavior norms. In small cohorts, leaders worked to identify their top few behaviors for each switch. Then they came together as a full leadership team to consolidate their lists and agree on a set of norms for their school district. Here's what they came up with:

- Be fully present in the moment.
- Seek input and collaborate.
- Own it and learn from it.
- Follow through.

Once they committed to these norms, the norms were published district-wide for all employees to see.

Leaders met with their staff to share these commitments and ask for their employees' help in adhering to the norms. In the spirit of struggling with, the leaders didn't try to impose the norms on their staff. Rather, they made a public commitment to these norms and asked their teams to help them, provide feedback, and hold them accountable.

New initiatives are often conceived in a vacuum and imposed on employees without their input or participation. This superintendent wanted to turn things upside down. His intention was for leaders to role model Compassionate Accountability first, ask for help from their teams, and give the initiative time to take effect.

The two-year leadership program includes four phases, each with specific behavioral goals. All district staff are surveyed after each phase to check if they are observing new behaviors and the impact they are having. Going to the next phase is contingent on leaders consistently exhibiting the target behaviors and those behaviors being experienced by their staff.

This process is consistent with the superintendent's vision to change culture by changing leadership behavior and accumulating stories of success that progressively transform the cultural narrative.

What You Can Do

Here are some ideas of what you can do to activate your compassion mindset:

- Develop behavior norms (see chapter 7). This can be a foundational exercise to solidify how you want to show up in your workplace.
- Don't try to implement large-scale behavior change until leaders are consistently modeling the change they want to see. This builds trust and shows integrity.
- Ask for input and support from your employees. Change is hard, and you will need all the help you can get. Be transparent and vulnerable about your efforts, and let your people tell you how you are doing, hold you accountable, and support you along the way.

Case Study 3

This case study shows how city leaders used Compassionate Accountability with the local government to enhance trust and collaboration. Working relationships between city leaders and local government are critical and can sometimes be difficult. Several years ago, the city administrator of my hometown and his team wanted to strengthen relationships with city commissioners to foster a more trusting and collaborative work environment. Relationships were strained at times, which led to unnecessary conflict and interfered with getting work done. They were spending too much time putting out fires, anticipating resistance, and defending themselves. They wanted to change the culture and narrative.

We helped them assess areas of most risk for negative conflict and where they had opportunities to bring Compassionate Accountability into the relationship. Over several years, they implemented communication strategies aimed at turning on the three switches:

- Proactively affirm the value and contribution of the commissioners. This demonstrated goodwill and positive intentions.
- Be more proactive with sharing information and seeking input from commissioners. This demonstrated transparency around information and a collaborative spirit.
- Establish clear boundaries and expectations around how information would flow and how they would report on city business during public commission meetings. This demonstrated courage and integrity, which built trust.

Their efforts paid off in terms of more positive relationships, less stress and anxiety during commission meetings, and a more collaborative approach to getting tasks done. One of the best outcomes was that as the public experienced more positive interactions, it motivated better candidates to run for office.

Last year our new city manager took it one step further. She asked county commissioners to join city staff for a joint training around communication and healthy conflict skills. All agreed and participated. For two days, we explored new ways to affirm each others' value, capability, and responsibility to elevate the impact and reputation of the work these leaders are doing in our community. The rapport, mutual respect, and gratitude was evident. It's been a win for these public servants and a win for the city that creates positive momentum.

What You Can Do

Change starts within each of us. Here are some ideas of what you can do to activate your compassion mindset. Take matters into your own hands, focus on what you can control, and change the way you communicate:

- Use the Compassionate Accountability Assessment to identify behaviors that are lacking and can be implemented to turn on your switches. Remember that each switch is necessary but not sufficient on its own to embody Compassionate Accountability.
- Be proactive instead of reactive. Don't wait until a conflict or crisis comes up. Implementing new habits in crisis situations is extremely difficult. Trying new things when the stakes are lower can help build confidence for the more difficult situations.

Case Study 4

This case study shows how one hospital replaced progressive discipline with Compassionate Accountability to pursue high reliability. The chief human resource officer (CHRO) of a regional healthcare system is helping transform his hospital into a high reliability organization using the principles of Compassionate Accountability. A high reliability organization has predictable and repeatable systems that support consistent operations while catching and correcting potentially catastrophic errors before they happen. Reaching this level of clinical and operational excellence often requires cultural transformation, fundamentally changing the attitudes, beliefs, goals, and values of the organization.

The leadership team of this hospital identified that the key to this journey was the creation of a safe environment. To reach a goal of zero errors, all employees needed to trust leadership to be able to report mistakes, close calls, systemic problems, policies that are not comprehensive, procedures that are not followed, performance that is suboptimal, and behavior that is counter to reliability without fear of punishment.

The CHRO recognized that the existing model of progressive discipline did not create a safe environment to speak up and actually worked against their goals. He became convinced that the principles of Compassionate Accountability could provide the fundamental shift needed to move in the right direction.

Executive leadership and key stakeholders identified four conditions made possible by Compassionate Accountability that they believed could move the needle:

- *Extension of grace and empathy*—Don't assume intent.
- *Exceptional listening*—Listen to understand, not respond.
- *Curiosity*—Ask questions, explore options.
- *Vulnerable communication*—Share feelings in a safe space.

This new structure was a big departure from the old pattern of progressive discipline, which led to fear, punitive action, judgment, blame, and alienation. The CHRO set about orienting his leaders in this new framework and training them in some new tools for dealing with errors in a different way. They addressed two important areas with a new framework: conversation and intervention.

First they focused on conversation. The first step any time someone comes forward to report something out of the ordinary is to engage in constructive and safe dialogue that affirms the employee's honesty, engages them around ideas to fix the problem, and keeps focus on the core value of quality. The outcome of these conversations is documented as an action plan with accountabilities and is given to the employee. Note how this conversation template reinforces value, capability, and responsibility at the same time.

Then they addressed intervention. Three types of interventions match the three types of errors that an employee might make. For natural human errors that aren't intentional, leaders are trained to console and offer support. For errors that put someone at risk, leaders should have a discussion about the situation. For clearly reckless behavior, leaders enforce appropriate consequences to keep people safe. Note how interventions are aimed at trusting intentions (value), learning from mistakes (capability), and ensuring safety (responsibility).

So far, results have been promising. The hospital is seeing increased reporting of issues, including what they call *near misses* and *good catches*. Both of these reflect increased safety to report and grassroots ownership over quality. They have discovered and corrected policies that contradict each other and procedures that put staff in situations where chance of errors is increased. Instead of having three different codes of conduct for various professional groups, the hospital has developed a single code of behavior for any staff member who enters the building. Most encouraging is a sense of shared accountability and pride among all levels when it comes to reporting to state and local regulatory agencies. The emerging picture is one of greater openness and shared responsibility.

The next step will be implementing consistent metrics. The CHRO is researching best practice metrics for high reliability organizations and consulting with his teams on how to begin measuring and tracking progress.

Recently I spoke with the chief quality officer about how their new approach is working. He shared that the biggest challenge is convincing employees that coming forward is safe. It's hard for them to believe since this new framework is so different from the way they used to work. "But the word is getting out that we mean what we say, so momentum is building," he added.

What You Can Do

Here are some ideas of what you can do to activate your compassion mindset:

- Identify a foundational process or outcome that, if improved, would make the biggest difference in your organization's success. For a hospital, consistently reducing errors and improving quality are fundamental to its success. An amusement park might focus on the customer experience and receiving five out of five stars on its surveys. What is it for your organization?
- Once you've identified what you want to improve, evaluate it through the lens of Compassionate Accountability. Most likely, the biggest threats to your goal come from our-switch-is-off behaviors. Review these behaviors in chapters 4–6, and see if you can make any connections.
- Next, evaluate the switch-is-on behaviors to see if any of these, if more prevalent, would help you move the needle toward your goal. Your biggest goals can be achieved by making sure the conditions support the outcomes you want.
- Begin to orient people to these new behaviors like the CHRO in this case study.
- I've said it before—make sure leaders are modeling the behaviors they want to see. This organization didn't even try to

implement a new paradigm until leaders were doing it. Even then, employees had a hard time believing it was for real.

- What gets measured gets done. Implement metrics to show progress. Connect those metrics to the target compassion mindset behaviors.

I hope these case studies give you a flavor for the many ways organizations can begin building their culture of Compassionate Accountability and offer you some practical ways you can take the next step. For additional resources, visit CompassionateAccountabilityBook.com.

Compassionate Accountability Can Change the World

My vision and dream is for Compassionate Accountability to find its way into every interaction in families, communities, organizations, and beyond. Imagine what the world could look like if the three switches of the compassion mindset were turned on in these situations.

Politics

I envision a world where politicians separate the person from the behavior and stop making the personal attacks. Our country is founded on the principle that human beings are innately valuable. Let's keep our value switch on. If politicians kept their capability switch on, they would recognize that diversity of thought and opinion is what makes us great. They would look for opportunities to bring together diverse viewpoints to create something new and better instead of attacking and belittling anyone who disagrees with them. They wouldn't disagree less, they would disagree better. By keeping their responsibility switch on, they would show what true integrity and courage looks like, taking full responsibility for their own actions instead of making excuses and denying reality. They would model what they believe instead of being self-righteously condescending toward anyone who dissents while doing the opposite behind closed doors. They would serve their country instead of their pocketbook.

Restorative Justice

I envision a world where justice means keeping our switches on while we make our communities safe. In this world we seek to be effective instead of being justified. In case study 4, when the hospital system replaced progressive discipline with Compassionate Accountability, the world didn't lapse into chaos. Just the opposite. That's because they kept their switches on while keeping their top priority: safety. Instead of moralizing and judging people, they focus on learning from mistakes. Instead of making decisions in an ivory tower, they involve those most impacted to be part of the solution. Instead of questioning intentions, they check assumptions and take it from there. When the value switch is on, we can address behavior directly while respecting the human being behind the behavior.

Climate Change

I'm not here to argue about what caused the climate crisis or whether we can turn it around. The reality is that it's here, and it's real. The question is, What do we do now? David Katz, whom you will read about in chapter 10, is founder of Plastic Bank, a global network of local recycling markets that empower the poor to transcend poverty by cleaning the environment. David kept his switches on in his effort to reduce pollution caused by plastic. He doesn't judge or diminish people or point fingers. Plastic Bank truly embodies the notion that people are valuable, capable, and responsible and that the best solutions emerge when we practice Compassionate Accountability.

With the value switch on, we would affirm the human experience of climate change, show empathy for those most affected, and join alongside them to understand the impact in their lives. With the capability switch on, we would seek to understand rather than push our own convenient theories and agendas. We would look for grassroots solutions that have the lowest or negative carbon footprints. We would include those most impacted in finding solutions that they can live with and implement. With our responsibility switch on, we would remind ourselves that no matter what happened before, we are each 100 percent responsible for what we do next. We would stop pointing fingers and instead focus on solutions. We would hold each other accountable for practices and policies that degrade our environment. We would focus on the most important goal: building a world that works for all.

Diversity, Equity, and Inclusion

Diversity is part of the grand design of the universe. Without diversity, we couldn't survive and thrive. Yet diversity is the root of conflict because it means we will look, act, and sound different. If diversity has a positive purpose, then the conflict caused by diversity must also have a positive purpose. I shared this quote from Michael Meade in my book *Conflict without Casualties*, and I've become more convinced that it's true: *"The purpose of conflict is to create."*

Conflict is our greatest source of energy. We get to choose how we use it. When we misuse that energy, it mutates into drama. But we can react in another way by using the energy of conflict to create. The highest aspirations of DEI should be to utilize the energy of conflict, generated by diversity, to create something new and better. This transcends and includes notions of tolerating or celebrating diversity, and moves to a place of leveraging diversity for the greater good.

How can we do this? Compassionate Accountability. Compassion is what makes us human, brings us together, and gets us back on track when we lose our way. Compassion is the ultimate gift we've been given as humans because it provides the antidote to drama and is the key for transforming conflict into a creative force.

I believe that Compassionate Accountability should be our attitude in how we approach DEI. No DEI effort or initiative is sufficient
unless it affirms and uplifts human value, capability, and responsibility.
Not just one component, but all of them. No DEI effort or initiative is
sufficient unless the three switches are on for everyone, not just some.
When we approach diversity with our compassion mindset activated,
we can create a better world that works for all.

Start Your Journey Today!

We've assembled a suite of support resources to extend the value of this
book and help you along the way. Visit CompassionateAccountability
Book.com to see what's available. If you want help on the journey, we
are here, because you are valuable, capable, and responsible.

Main Points

- Compassionate Accountability is not another program but a
  mindset, skill set, and framework for struggling with others in any
  situation.
- Compassionate Accountability is not another training but a foundational set of principles and practices for thriving work cultures.
- Compassionate Accountability is not another prescription for difficult conversations but a template to engage differently for transformative results.
- Compassionate Accountability is not another theory but an actionable process for mindfulness, social and emotional intelligence, leadership agility, inclusion, presence, healthy conflict, and resiliency.

PART IV

OVERCOMING BARRIERS TO COMPASSION

CHAPTER 9

COMPASSION IS JUST FOR BLEEDING HEARTS

"DO I HAVE to be an emotional bleeding heart to practice compassion?"

"How can I help even if I'm not a touchy-feely person?"

"Will I have to change who I am to be more compassionate?"

Can you relate to any of these questions? If so, this chapter is for you.

Here's the reality and what this chapter is all about: *Empathy isn't the only motivator for compassion. Different people have their own reasons for acting compassionately, and they do it in different ways.*

One of the most common definitions of compassion can be summarized like this: compassion is empathy in action.

Compassion is not the same as empathy or altruism, though the concepts are related. While empathy refers more generally to our ability to take the perspective of and feel the emotions of another person, compassion is when those feelings and thoughts include the desire to help. In this definition, empathy and altruism are the instigators and motivators. Taking the next step to help is the action part. This definition is promoted by some of the most prominent compassion research entities, such as Stanford University's Center for Compassion and Altruism Research. His Holiness the Dalai Lama is one of their subject matter experts.

Defining compassion as empathy in action limits our understanding and practice of compassion, particularly in a workplace setting for leaders. It assumes that the emotional experience of empathy is the only precursor and motivator for compassion.

Many Reasons and Many Ways to Act Compassionately

Empathy is a fundamental and critical human experience. In fact, empathy is baked into our biology. Mirror neurons, first discovered in the 1990s, are a type of brain cell that responds equally when we perform an action and when we witness someone else perform the same action.[1] Emotion researchers believe this type of neuron is the biological basis of empathy. Because humans are a social species, we rely on the ability to relate to what others are experiencing. This allows us to support each other in many ways, including coming to the aid of our fellow humans in times of suffering and crisis. Even Charles Darwin, who's best known for the concept of survival of the fittest, concluded that species who affiliate and support each other through tough times are more likely to be more successful. Empathy is key to our survival.

Try telling this to an overworked leader struggling to survive at a high-stakes job in an uncertain job market. Empathy is the last thing on their mind, and they would not feel comfortable embracing it. From where they stand, the key to survival is innovation, drive, bold courage, and opportunism. They're not a bleeding heart! Empathy is not the key to their survival in their world. Ironically, I'm guessing many leaders reading this book can empathize.

In our experience working with leaders who need to develop more compassion, starting with a definition grounded in empathy is a tough pill to swallow. This doesn't mean that they don't need to be kinder or more thoughtful or consider the experience of others besides themselves. Perhaps it means that empathy can't be the only on-ramp to compassionate behavior.

I've met many leaders who act compassionately but show little empathy. Furthermore, they would reject the notion that empathy motivates their behavior. They take plenty of action to help and support others, but it's not because they feel for or feel with the people they are leading. They aren't bleeding hearts.

How do we validate this experience while helping these leaders develop a fuller understanding and practice of compassion?

Our work with personality diversity has opened up new perspectives for us and our clients on what motivates people into compassionate action.[2] The Process Communication Model® (PCM), developed by psychologist Dr. Taibi Kahler, identifies six clusters of psychological needs that motivate behavior.[3] Each cluster is tied to one of six distinct personality types in each of us, called a *phase type*. We all have all six, arranged in a preferred, set order. But at any given time in our lives, one of these six is primary in terms of our current source of motivation. Kahler's research also showed that each of the six types has a preferred frame of reference, or perception, through which they take in and process the world. These perceptions strongly influence how we experience the world, including our relationships and connection with others.[4]

When personality is viewed as types *in* people instead of types *of* people, we can see that it has strong connections to empathy and compassion. If I have all six types in me, then I have the capability of experiencing and appreciating all six types in you. As a leader, my desire and capability to act compassionately toward others is dependent on my ability to experience and appreciate your strongest type within me, even if that's not my strongest type. Conversely, how I understand and experience compassion personally is strongly related to the relative strength of the different types in me. One size doesn't fit all, and there's not one single pathway to compassion.

I trust that people reading this book might vary in their capacity to demonstrate compassion, but at least they know it matters. Most leaders we work with don't dispute the data showing that more compassionate leadership and workplace cultures can lead to better business results.

These leaders have two important questions though: Why? and How?

Those who promote compassion as empathy in action would probably answer, "Because you care, show caring."

This answer is insufficient and unhelpful. Many leaders can't relate to this and consequently don't engage to develop their skills. That's because compassion is motivated by much more than empathy.

Table 9.1 explores the six PCM personality types, looking at their psychological motivators, their communication currency, and how these motivators influence their capacity to perform compassionate acts.

Note: Why and how each type acts compassionately are not part of the PCM model and have been added for this book with the approval of Taibi Kahler and Kahler Communications Inc.

Each personality type is motivated to act compassionately in different ways, and the way in which each type shows it looks different as well. At the risk of offending the altruism researchers, table 9.1 clearly shows that compassionate acts have some level of a "What's in it for me" mentality built in. I suppose you could argue that some psychological motivators are more altruistic than others, but fundamentally, a psychological need is an inborn, individual craving that must be met to function productively and stay healthy. The notion that compassion might not be fully altruistic will be addressed in chapter 12 when I unpack the misconception that compassion is for selfless servant leaders.

TABLE 9.1. PCM personality phase types, psychological needs, communication currencies, and compassion behaviors

PCM phase type	Psychological motivators	Communication currency	Why would I act compassionately?	How would I act compassionately?
Harmonizer	Recognition of person, sensory	Compassion	I care about people and want them to be happy and get along.	I show empathy, care, kindness, and acts of love.
Rebel	Contact	Humor	Acting compassionately is fun, and we get to play together.	I play with you and come up with creative solutions.
Thinker	Recognition of productive work and time structure	Logic	Acting compassionately makes sense, saves time and money, and increases productivity.	I design better solutions to help you be more productive.
Imaginer	Solitude	Imagination	Acting compassionately removes barriers and opens up new possibilities.	I create an open, nonjudgmental space for innovation.
Persister	Recognition of principled work, recognition of conviction	Values	Acting compassionately is the right thing to do and aligns with our values.	I advocate for what's right, keeping our principles in the foreground.
Promoter	Incidence—a lot of excitement in a short period of time	Initiative	Acting compassionately increases buy-in and gets things moving quicker.	I use charisma to get everyone moving in the same direction.

Full compassion has affective, cognitive, and behavioral components. It requires feeling with and for each other, cognitively understanding what's going on and seeking solutions, and upholding core principles through our behaviors. The importance lies in how three facets of compassion connect to different motivators and, in turn, where each person can most naturally start their journey toward a fuller understanding and practice of compassion.

For example, the harmonizer type in us can easily make the emotional connection to others' experiences and respond to the urge to make things better. "My heart goes out to you, and I want to help." About 30 percent of the population has harmonizer as their strongest personality type. This most closely parallels the popular definition of compassion as empathy in action.

For the thinker type in us, the holy grail is productivity. This type is stirred to improve effectiveness and efficiency. If we want inclusion, they will research the best practices, identify how our processes and procedures need to be modified, and implement the metrics to show progress. This would be a tremendous contribution to building a more inclusive work culture—an equally valuable manifestation of compassion, albeit a very cognitive one. About 25 percent of the population has thinker as their strongest personality type.

The persister type in us is activated by inconsistencies between values and behaviors: how we believe people should be treated and how they are actually being treated. Persister values and principles are the beacon guiding them toward actions that increase quality, dignity, justice, equity, inclusion, or safety. Don't confuse their passion for empathy though. The emotions they experience and express are an indication of their commitment, not their connection. Walking the talk is their specialty, a behavioral manifestation of compassion. About 10 percent of the population has persister as their strongest personality type.

Here's an example of someone who was motivated to act compassionately from a more persister and thinker vantage point.

Dr. Tahira Reid Smith is a mechanical engineering professor who spent more than a decade at Purdue University, where she was the first Black woman to earn tenure at the School of Mechanical Engineering in 2018. In fall 2020, she was a NASA visiting scholar and joined the mechanical engineering and engineering design faculty at Penn State University in 2023.

The notion that mechanical engineers do not factor compassion in their work is a stereotype. Tahira exemplifies a more accurate portrayal of how a mechanical engineer might infuse their compassionate motivations in their work. Her unique perspective and cultural background has allowed her to incorporate these influences into her work. For instance, growing up caring for diabetic grandparents gave her a heightened awareness of the needs of the elderly and those struggling with their health. She later learned of the challenges faced by survivors of breast cancer as they interacted with mammogram machines and by cancer patients receiving radiation treatment.

As Tahira observed the discomfort, loss of dignity, and anxiety that so many patients experience while interacting with medical devices, she was motivated to do something about it. "I like to address human centered problems that matter," she told me in an interview.[5] Tahira has pioneered the engineering subspecialty called *compassionate design*. Her focus is in helping preserve dignity and comfort for patients who interact with medical devices. This framework inspires engineers to be more intentional about mitigating design features that could negatively impact one's dignity, sense of security, and their ability to be empowered.

Tahira loves to speak to children, hoping to inspire the next generation of compassionate design engineers. She tells them, "No matter where you are from or who you are, none of it is a waste. All of it has the ability, with the right education and training, to make a difference. Who you are influences how you approach your work."

Tahira's commitment to bring dignity to women, coupled with a brilliant technical mind, motivated her toward being a leader in the field of medical device development. For her, compassion is about making a difference in the world by leveraging her technical capabilities.

I hope this illustrates how compassionate acts are not necessarily predicated on empathy, or at least not just emotional empathy. *Anyone can be compassionate, but not everyone is stirred by emotions alone,* and that's okay. Many leaders who were born with fewer mirror neurons than Mother Teresa will hopefully find this message encouraging.

When I ask people to describe what compassion looks like in action, a common phrase I hear is "Meet people where they are." What if we applied that principle to how we teach compassion to others?

It works. Making compassion accessible to anyone starts with recognizing that different people have different motivational needs and then affirming those needs as a foundation for compassionate behavior. Our strategy for building compassion in leaders starts with three fundamental questions: (1) What would a more compassionate workplace look like? (2) How are you motivated to help make that happen, and (3) What can you contribute to support those outcomes?

Interestingly, when we meet people where they are, they are more likely to journey with us into new places and take risks to expand their compassion perspectives and skill sets. It's a win-win.

Affective versus Cognitive Empathy

I, like most people, often consider empathy as an affective experience. We experience emotions about what others are going through, and these emotions get our attention. For many people, though, these emotions can become overwhelming. When we experience and take on other people's suffering, it can lead to empathy fatigue. This happens often among helping professionals in the mental health and healthcare industries. Emotional empathy alone can take a toll on us.

Empathy is more than most people realize, though. It's not just affective, it's also cognitive. Kristen Donnelly is an international empathy

educator and researcher with two decades of experience helping people understand the beauty in difference and the power in inclusivity.
From her research, she has concluded that you can't universally associate empathy with emotions, but you can universally associate empathy
with understanding. The practice of empathy requires cultivating cognitive skills for better understanding ourselves and others.

Kristen maintains that empathy is a mindset that reframes how we
think about ourselves and others. We make a decision to get curious
and learn about others' perspectives and experiences. By doing this,
we remind ourselves that not only are we allowed to be human, but we
have to be human. Cognitive empathy reminds us we are full, messy,
imperfect, and wonderful humans. It helps us avoid what Kristen calls
"summarizing people," which is the foundation of stereotyping and
dehumanizing.[6]

Cognitive empathy is a mindset and a choice. It involves learning
about what others are experiencing, understanding their perspective
and perceptions, and learning what makes them tick. The Golden Rule
says, "Treat others as you want to be treated." Traditional affective
empathy might lead us in this direction. But cognitive empathy helps
us transcend our mirror neurons so we can recognize that people aren't
all just like us. This helps us implement the Platinum Rule: "Treat others as *they* want to be treated."

Compassion is more than empathy in action. It's about being motivated in many different ways to make a positive difference in each others' lives by using our inborn strengths as a starting point.

Main Points

- *The barrier*—Defining compassion as empathy in action is limiting
  and creates barriers to entry for many leaders. They can't embrace
  empathy as the on-ramp for developing compassion even though
  they support a more compassionate workplace.

- *The reality*—Empathy isn't the only motivator for compassion. Different people have their own reasons for acting compassionately, and they do it in different ways. Furthermore, empathy has a cognitive component, so we can appreciate another's experience and meet people where they are by using our heads, not just our hearts.
- *The hopeful message*—Anyone can find an on-ramp to expand their understanding and practice of compassion.
- *The lesson*—If we are trying to become more compassionate leaders, we must meet people where they are and invite them to make a positive difference by using their inborn motivators and strengths as a starting point.
- *The leadership accountability*—You are accountable for being a good steward of your personality, skills, and experience. As a leader, you are accountable for helping others become good stewards of their personality, skills, and experiences. Although you aren't responsible for their behaviors, you are accountable to them for your behaviors, which means meeting them where they are, honoring who they are, and journeying together to a better future. That's compassion: struggling with.

CHAPTER 10

COMPASSION CREATES DEPENDENCE

"HOW DO I help when I can't fix the problem?"

"How can I help while fostering self-sufficiency and independence?"

"How do I prevent burnout when faced with pain and suffering every day?"

Can you relate to any of these questions? If so, this chapter is for you.

Here's the reality and what this chapter is all about: *compassion actually means to "suffer with." When we view compassion as an opportunity to get alongside people and walk together through the pain, we can find solutions that transform everyone involved in the relationship.*

Here's a more detailed version of the definition of compassion that I shared in the last chapter: compassion is the feeling that arises when you are confronted with another's suffering and are motivated to relieve that suffering. This definition involves a big misconception: that the goal of compassion is to alleviate suffering.

Suffering is everywhere. Poverty, injustice, natural disasters, war, and the list goes on. When people are hurting, humans naturally want to help alleviate that suffering, which is good. Think of all the positive changes that have happened in our world because people stepped up and took action to alleviate suffering.

The main problem with assuming that the goal of compassion is to alleviate suffering is that it is one-sided. This assumption can drive leadership behaviors that create dependence and lead to burnout.

The Latin root of the word *compassion* means "to suffer or struggle with." Stated another way, compassion is about suffering alongside another person. It doesn't mean "to take away the suffering."

These are fundamentally different mindsets about the goal of compassion, and they make a huge difference in how leaders approach it.

Alleviating Suffering Can Create Dependence

My parents were unconventional missionaries. They weren't preachers, and they didn't seek converts. They wanted to make a difference, but they had observed the consequences of helping with the goal of alleviating suffering specifically. They saw the negative impact of outsiders swooping in with all the answers, often implementing inappropriate solutions that created dependence rather than empowerment. That's not compassion.

The desire to alleviate suffering often motivates short-term fixes with unintended consequences. My father told me stories of efforts to make circumstances better for residents that backfired in the long run. One example was a dam with a waterwheel that would pump water up the hill to the village so that people could have easier access to water. It seemed like a great idea to alleviate the suffering of having to carry water up the hill. The unintended consequences were that damming the river ended up flooding important farmland. Also, the waterwheel and pump often broke down, and parts had to be shipped from America or Europe, so for long periods of time, the system didn't work.

My mother was a nurse and focused a lot of her time in rural Congo providing care and education for pre- and postnatal health issues. At that time, Nestlé was heavily promoting dried milk products to mothers, advertising that they could have a ready source of nutrition for their babies any time they wanted, and it didn't need refrigeration. What Nestlé failed to account for was that breast milk is sterile, but reconstituting dried milk requires clean water. Furthermore, breast-feeding helps reduce the chance of getting pregnant, so switching from breast milk to formula increases the chance of unwanted pregnancy. My mom worked to provide education and support for mothers to end their dependence on Nestlé formula and evaluate the most sustainable and empowering solutions to their real-life challenges.

My father introduced rabbits to the region. As I mentioned in the introduction, he grew up a farmer in rural Kansas. He went to school to study agriculture and livestock. The problem he sought to address was a lack of sustainable and affordable protein in tropical climates. Local residents had an ample supply of fruits and root vegetables high in starch but protein in the form of meat was expensive. The result was a high incidence of malnutrition and associated health problems.

Rabbits proved to be a promising solution. All dark meat, high in protein, and feasting on anything green, rabbits seemed like a good fit. People commonly owned chickens, but eating a chicken was a special treat. By spending time learning and living with local residents, my father helped codevelop a way of raising rabbits in elevated hutches made of wire mesh. With an abundant supply of greens for the rabbits, people had no problem keeping them fed. Rabbit manure, less danger-ous to plants than chicken manure if not composted properly, could be collected and used as fertilizer for crops. Whatever food fell through the elevated mesh hutches would be scavenged by the chickens. And rabbits breed, well, like rabbits. This solution was sustainable, or what my dad called *appropriate technology*.

Thirty years after leaving Congo, my father returned to visit. At the time, he was battling prostate cancer and knew his time was limited. He wanted to return to this formative place and time in his life. He made the trip with my brother, his eldest son, who was just a teenager back in the 1970s, and my brother's son, his grandson. Three generations traveled back to reconnect and find closure. Although much had changed, one thing hadn't. The locals were still raising rabbits, which were still an integral part of their ecosystem. They welcomed my father like a chief in the village. They were so proud to show him how they'd continued and evolved the appropriate technology of rabbits, and he felt so proud to have been part of something that increased capability, dignity, and sustainability instead of dependence.

When I was practicing therapy as a clinical psychologist, I learned a valuable lesson about change. My patients didn't come to me because they wanted to change. They came to me because they wanted the pain to go away. As a young, inexperienced therapist, I didn't recognize the difference. Early on I often got hooked into trying to fix my patients, offering solutions that I thought could alleviate the suffering and then getting frustrated with them when they didn't do as I suggested. I'd try to persuade them to change their behavior and then describe them as *noncompliant* or *resistant to change* in the medical chart when they didn't follow through. I kept doing it, though, because patients would praise me for being so smart and helpful, even when they weren't doing what I recommended. I felt needed and valued, even though I wasn't being effective.

Laurel Donnellan is the founder of Compassionate Leaders Circle and a regular contributor to *Forbes* magazine, featuring leaders who are pioneering what it means to be compassionate at work. She shared this philosophy with me for how she approaches her coaching practice with compassion: "I can't want something to change for clients more than they want it."[1] It took me a while to learn this lesson for myself.

I became a much happier therapist when I realized that meeting people where they are and struggling with them to find their own solutions was a much more effective long-term strategy. In fact, the more I walked with my patients through their pain, the more they started to figure out their own solutions. The upside was better clinical outcomes. They needed support and someone to believe in them. Simply validating a person's experience and getting out of their way is sometimes the best intervention.

Whenever we begin a training or consulting relationship with leaders, we share a list of ten permissions. These permissions are designed to help affirm the essential value, capability, and responsibility of each person in the relationship and offer a framework for a positive working relationship.[2] One of the permissions says, "It's okay to want others to learn and grow without expecting them to." This one is particularly challenging and important for me. As a learning and development professional, I come with lots of experience and solutions that I believe can alleviate my clients' suffering. It's easy for me to get attached to these solutions for my clients. The danger of this habit is that I might not invest the time and energy to learn about what they are actually struggling with and what they bring to the table as resources to solve the problem. If I get invested in alleviating their suffering, I set up a no-win situation. If it goes well, I can take all the credit. If it goes bad, I can blame them for not doing it right or being lazy.

Have you ever met a consultant like this? I have. In fact, when we started Next Element, one thing we promised ourselves was to avoid creating dependence. We didn't want to be like those other consultants and trainers who positioned themselves as the savior and made their clients dependent on them. This business model is lucrative in the short term but destined to fail in the long run. This practice is called *rescuing* and is part of the energy-sucking dynamics of drama.[3] That's not compassion.

In most corporate workplaces, leaders are set up to become rescuers via the dynamic called the Peter principle; they are promoted to their level of incompetence. We often tell newly promoted leaders, *"Before you were a leader, your success depended on your ability to solve problems and produce. Now your success depends on your ability to help others solve their own problems and produce."*

The person who is best at alleviating suffering is often the one who gets promoted. We promote people who are great problem-solvers and take initiative with their solutions. Without awareness or training in how to actually lead people, they do more of what they are good at:

- They make a living off of fixing everybody else's problems.
- They have an attitude of superiority, as if they know what's best for others.
- They thrive on being the one with all the answers.
- They adopt the belief that "I'm worthwhile, but you're worthwhile only if you take my advice and appreciate it."

This type of leadership creates dependence and resentment, squashes innovation, and lowers engagement.

Employees don't benefit from leaders who take away the suffering. They need leaders who come alongside them to understand the struggle and support value, capability, and responsibility.

Alleviating Suffering Can Lead to Burnout

According to the World Health Organization, burnout is a syndrome resulting from workplace stress that has not been successfully managed. This state is characterized by three dimensions: feelings of energy depletion or exhaustion, increased mental distance from one's job or feelings of negativism or cynicism related to one's job, and reduced professional efficacy.[4]

According to the American Psychological Association's *2021 Work and Well-Being Survey* of 1,501 US adult workers, 79 percent of employees had experienced work-related stress in the month before the survey. Although stress itself isn't always negative, it can have negative consequences when it becomes chronic or severe or when people don't perceive that they have a way out. Nearly three in five employees reported negative impacts of work-related stress, including lack of interest, motivation, or energy (26 percent) and lack of effort at work (19 percent). Meanwhile, 36 percent reported cognitive weariness, 32 percent reported emotional exhaustion, and an astounding 44 percent reported physical fatigue—a 38 percent increase since 2019.[5] Global employee wellness research conducted by the global management consulting firm McKinsey & Company indicated that in 2022 49 percent of employees felt at least somewhat burned out.[6]

Certain industries, such as healthcare, have been hit especially hard. In 2019 the National Academy of Medicine reported that burnout had reached "crisis" levels, with up to 54 percent of nurses and physicians and up to 60 percent of medical students and residents suffering from burnout.[7] The COVID-19 pandemic has since affected the mental health of health workers nationwide, with more than 50 percent of public health workers reporting symptoms of at least one mental health condition, such as anxiety, depression, and increased levels of posttraumatic stress disorder.

Interestingly, during this same time period, the public perceived a reduction in compassion in healthcare. Drs. Stephen Trzeciak and Anthony Mazzarelli reviewed over 1,000 abstracts and 280 scientific studies on the role of compassion in healthcare. One of their most significant findings is that nearly half of all Americans believe that the US healthcare system and healthcare providers are not compassionate.

Physicians routinely miss emotional cues from patients and actually miss 60 to 90 percent of opportunities to respond to patients with compassion, which can be something as simple as validating a patient's feelings, telling them you care, and offering support.[8]

What's the solution? Stephen and Anthony's findings suggest that the solution might involve a reimagined understanding and practice of compassion that goes beyond the assumption of alleviating suffering. They found that physicians who measured lower in compassion were more likely to experience burnout. In contrast to the destructive effects of empathy fatigue and depersonalization, compassion actually increased resilience and wellness among caregivers.

How can engaging more with patients help reduce burnout? The answer brings us back to the first misconception of compassion predicated on empathy. Neuroscience data supports a distinction between empathy and compassion. Functional magnetic resonance imaging scans show that empathy activates the pain centers of the brain. Over time, this takes a toll and can be one of the causes of burnout. Consequently, it may explain why burnout involves feelings of cynicism and negativity and emotional distancing as a mode of coping. *Compassion fatigue* is a misnomer. It should be called *empathy fatigue*. Burnout is accelerated when we take on and carry too much of other people's suffering for too long without being able to make it go away.

The good news is that compassion activates the reward centers of the brain. When physicians are taught basic techniques to actively engage in constructive problem-solving with patients, they feel more energized and optimistic. Rather than feeling hopeless and cynical from taking on so much pain and not being able to alleviate all the suffering, they feel more effective and helpful.

Leaning in with compassion is more healthy than checking out.

In healthcare, the explicit goal and expectation is to alleviate physical suffering. The problem is, life is messy, and so many problems don't have an easy fix. Leadership is no different. Wouldn't it be nice if every employee complaint, change management project, or conflict with a customer was as simple as resetting a broken bone and putting a cast on it? In leadership, like in medicine, most problems aren't understood or solved with simple technical or physical solutions. Heightened emotions, long-term habits, complicated relationships, hidden agendas, baggage from our past, unpredictable conditions, and a host of other factors can make most leadership challenges seem insurmountable.

When leaders expect themselves to have all the answers, solve all the problems, and alleviate all the suffering, it can be overwhelming. At least once a week, a leader discloses to me the expectations they put on themselves and how stressful the pressure is. They believe they are supposed to have it all figured out and come to the rescue with solutions that make everything better. They believe that not doing so would be perceived as weak and a sign of incompetence. This belief is particularly true for newly promoted leaders and leadership in turbulent times, so they take on the burden of suffering, often taking over responsibility from those who are most closely impacted and should be involved in the solution.

As my friend and leadership expert Ken Blanchard often says, "Those who plan the battle rarely battle the plan." As a leader, if you position yourself to plan all the battles, you will also spend a lot of time on the battlefield in power struggles with those who could be allies instead of adversaries.

If compassionate leadership means alleviating suffering, leaders can't survive for long. It's a recipe for burnout. They must have a better way.

The Game-Changing Impact of Struggling with Others

David Katz is the founder of Plastic Bank, an internationally recognized social enterprise offering a circular solution to ocean plastic.

Plastic Bank empowers a global network of recycling communities in vulnerable coastal areas to transcend poverty by stopping ocean-bound plastic. David's humanitarian work has earned him international recognition. He is the recipient of the United Nations Lighthouse award for Planetary Health, the Paris Climate Conference Sustainia Community Award, and the Ernst and Young Lifetime Achievement Award and was named the Entrepreneur Organization's Global Citizen.

David is a steward of the earth and a champion for the poor, and he's adamantly opposed to the notion that compassion is about alleviating suffering. David reassures people that nothing is wrong with seeking to reduce suffering in the world. The problem is how we go about it. Too many people and organizations approach the problem with one-sided solutions, swooping in to fix issues without understanding the problem or involving those who are suffering in being part of the solution. As David said, *"You can't donate the end of poverty."*

The solution is to struggle with people toward better solutions rather than trying to take away the pain. The long-term impact is that suffering is reduced. This approach is the essence of compassion.

The business model of Plastic Bank assumes that those who are suffering should be an active part of the solution. High rates of poverty often occur along coastal regions where pollution is highest. Plastic accumulates along beaches, especially where rivers meet the ocean. With Plastic Bank, David has linked the problem of plastic pollution with the problem of poverty to find a solution that empowers people to solve their own problems.

Local residents recycle plastic and receive credit toward education and other resources that help them work toward a better future. Plastic Bank partners with global businesses like S. C. Johnson and Procter & Gamble who have committed to use and pay competitive prices for recycled plastic.

This "struggling with" mindset embraces interdependence. These global companies make a commitment to use recycled plastic and pay competitive prices for it. This is their struggle. Participants in the Plastic Bank program invest their time and energy to collect plastic pollutants in exchange for opportunities to improve their earning potential. They also invest their time and energy to realize this potential through their own efforts. This is their struggle.

This business and mindset has multiple positive outcomes. Local residents achieve a higher standard of living, more confidence, and a sense of pride. Global companies contribute to reducing pollution and boost their public brand image. Highly polluted parts of the world get cleaned up. The overall demand for new plastic goes down, thus reducing the use of nonrenewable fossil fuels.

Plastic Bank's business model utilizes several principles that any leader can apply to increase compassion:

- Meet people where they are.
- Understand and leverage connections for a more systemic solution.
- Eliminate dependence on external inputs.
- Clarify that everyone has important responsibilities. Nobody gets a free ride, and everybody benefits.

The Gift of Struggle

Remember Bobby Herrera, cofounder and CEO of Populus Group, first introduced in chapter 3? As one of thirteen children in a migrant family, Bobby knows about struggling. He learned the value of hard work, rising early, and putting in long hours in the fields. After high school, boot camp became his ticket of opportunity. He is a proud Army veteran.

Bobby believes the biggest mistake people make is not sharing their story of struggle. Everyone has struggles that give them purpose and identity. At first, Bobby resisted sharing his story because he bought into a definition of compassion that included being strong for everyone else, having the answers, and alleviating suffering. But after Bobby shared his story, it transformed his company into a community. It connected people, and they began sharing their stories. It has created an empowering and attractive company culture at Populus Group.

Sharing our struggles feels vulnerable, and so often we don't want to show our cracks. What if someone can't relate to our struggle? What if they try to fix it without understanding it? In his book, *The Gift of Struggle*, Bobby reminds us that cracks are how the light gets in.[9] Sharing our struggles isn't about taking away the pain. It's about journeying through it together and recognizing the transformative impact of struggle in our lives. *How can someone struggle with us if they don't know what we are struggling with?* This doesn't mean you have to disclose your deepest personal secrets or confidential employee information. It means you let others know how you are doing with issues relevant to your relationship with them and your role as a leader.

Practicing Compassion Even When You Can't Fix a Problem

One of the biggest complaints we hear from employees is that their leaders don't understand or appreciate what they are dealing with. They don't feel heard.

Whether you are a nurse, parent, teacher, or manager, I'm guessing you desperately wish you could fix it all, make the pain go away, and make everyone's lives easier. Some leaders jump to the conclusion that they haven't done enough to fix the problems or that they've done all they know how and it's still not enough. Some employees make unrealistic demands based on the assumption that "you aren't paying me enough to put up with this." Neither of these attitudes lead to meaningful and lasting change because they don't address the real issue.

That doesn't mean you can't practice compassion. If compassion means struggling with others through tough times, this gives us new hope for how we can be compassionate even when alleviating suffering isn't in the cards. At times like this, maybe the best starting point is to meet people where they are, take the time to understand their struggles, and just be with them through it. If you jump too quickly to solutions, you miss the connection, learning, and transformation that happens in the struggle. Truly being with someone in their struggle can change everything. This approach is particularly applicable for some of the most challenging issues, such as diversity, equity, and inclusion. I might not be able to fix the problem of racism today, but I can come alongside people who are victims of discrimination to understand and validate the struggle. Maybe I can be an ally today and an advocate tomorrow, and together we can struggle toward evolving our work culture to be more inclusive.

Main Points

- *The barrier*—Assuming the goal of compassion is to alleviate suffering can lead to relationships based on rescuing, which creates dependence and leads to burnout.
- *The reality*—Compassion actually means to "suffer with." When we view compassion as an opportunity to get alongside people and walk together through the pain, we can find solutions that transform everyone involved in the relationship.
- *The hopeful message*—You no longer have to expect yourself to fix the problem to be compassionate. Anyone can practice compassion, even when alleviating the suffering isn't possible or the best long-term option.
- *The lesson*—The starting point for compassion is to get open with each other about what we are going through, and embrace the

gift of struggle. Even when we can't fix the pain, we can be with each other through it. This, by itself, can open up perspectives we never saw before and transform relationships and systems.

- *The leadership accountability*—You are accountable for connecting with people at a human level, and that includes sharing your struggles. Only then can you expect others to do the same. Being vulnerable isn't weak, and it isn't a liability if you take responsibility to treat your own and others' struggles with respect and kindness.

CHAPTER 11

COMPASSION IS SOFT

"HOW CAN I show compassion and not be seen as weak?"

"How can I care for people but also not let them walk all over me?"

"Real leadership requires hard skills. Compassion is a soft skill, right?"

Can you relate to any of these questions? If so, this chapter is for you.

Here's the reality and what this chapter is all about: *compassion requires the bravery to be vulnerable, the confidence to be humble, and the courage to walk the talk.*

Calling compassion *soft* is another way of saying it doesn't matter or isn't relevant to the real problems leaders are trying to solve. Compassion is often lumped in with all the other social and emotional soft skills as nice to have but not critical.

I'm not going to argue with this. Not because it doesn't matter but because that's not the purpose of this book. The evidence that compassion in leadership and at work matters is so overwhelming that I'm not going to spend energy on those who haven't bought into the idea yet.

I'll let marketing guru, culture expert, and noted ruckus-maker Seth Godin say it for me: "Let's call them real skills, not soft."[1]

Another meaning of *soft* in this context is that compassion is just touchy-feely emotional stuff. That's not true either, which was addressed in chapter 9.

What about the notion that compassion is soft, as in "not difficult"? Is compassion easy?

Jonathan Keyser is the founder and thought leader behind Keyser, one of the largest commercial real estate tenant brokerage firms in Arizona and one of the fastest-growing in the country. Jonathan grew up as the son of Christian missionary parents in Papua New Guinea. Returning to the United States as a young adult was the first time he realized he was poor. He didn't like it and wanted to be rich. Real estate gave him that path, so he went all in, learning from the best about how to be ruthless to get ahead. But after a while, he experienced an existential crisis, a point where he realized he had compromised his core values to achieve success. I had the opportunity to talk with Jonathan about his journey.[2]

After hearing a speaker talk about the selfless servant leadership model, he wondered if putting people and relationships first and still being financially successful was possible. He asked the speaker afterward how long it takes to achieve success with this philosophy and was told it would take five years to see results. That seemed like an eternity to Jonathan, but he was the kind of person who never backed down from a challenge and prided himself on exceeding expectations. He went all in again, made a 180-degree turn, and dedicated all his energy to helping others in his community. For several years, all he did was look for opportunities to help other people and organizations. Many, including Jonathan himself, were skeptical: "Many people thought I had hit my head." Despite his own misgivings, over time Jonathan began to experience the benefits. Leaders remembered his kindness when the time came that they needed real estate brokerage services.

COMPASSION IS SOFT   187

Others referred business to him because they trusted him. Kindness and compassion build trust. Trust opens doors.

But it wasn't that easy. During the ten years following Jonathan's big decision to practice compassion instead of being ruthless, he learned two important lessons about how hard it is: compassion is a mindset, not a tactic, and compassion is a choice, not a mandate.

Compassion Is a Mindset, Not a Tactic

The first lesson Jonathan learned is that a philosophy of helping others first is a fundamental mindset. It can't be seen as a tactic, short-term strategy, or quick fix. It's a change in how we view ourselves and others. We must hold this core value dear. It starts with a personal transformation. Jonathan describes having to come to a place in his heart that he actually wanted to "fall in love with people," truly looking for the value and potential in each human being with whom he made contact. This took a lot of time, energy, and personal work. He experienced a huge change when he went from seeing other people as a means to an end. This mindset allowed him to get curious with people, learning about their passions, dreams, gifts, and goals. This, in turn, gave him the insights to find meaningful and uplifting ways to help them without expecting anything in return. In my conversations with Jonathan, he reinforces over and over that a compassionate approach to others begins inside of us. If we don't change how we see ourselves and others, we can't change our relationships and results.

I have a natural aversion to the phrase *servant leadership*, especially when it includes the word *selfless*. Perhaps this is because of my personality, which tends toward opportunism on a good day, narcissism on a bad day. Or maybe it's because I've seen so many leaders serve selflessly until they burn out. Give until it hurts and until you break down. I want no part of that. We'll get to that in the next chapter. Every time I have a guest on my podcast who mentions servant leadership, I ask them this question: "What about taking care of ourselves? If selfless means we aren't caring for ourselves, what happens when our tank is empty?"

Compassion Is a Choice, Not a Mandate

Jonathan's answer to this question was the most satisfying and made the most sense to me of anything I've heard. A second lesson he learned while trying to implement a selfless servant leadership philosophy is that serving others is a choice, not a mandate.

Jonathan explained that this type of compassion works only when we make the choice to say yes, lean in, and serve others. This doesn't mean we change who we are meeting with or what we are working on, but it changes how we go about it. When we recognize that we have a choice, reality gets a lot more real and a lot more difficult. Nobody is making us do it. We have to own it. We can't blame anyone else or make excuses for our behavior. This intentionality in who we serve and how we serve gives our efforts a lot more purpose and direction. Purpose generates energy to sustain us. Mandates are draining and invite resistance and resentment.

Many people ask Jonathan, "So do you just say yes to everyone? Where do you draw the line?" He's very clear about this. You can't serve with an empty tank, so you have to be just as intentional with your boundaries as you are with your engagements with others. You can't say yes to every opportunity to help, or you'll have nothing left to give. And you can't take on everyone's suffering. This balance isn't easy to achieve though. As with any leader, Jonathan is pulled in many directions every day. But he maintains his enthusiasm and energy for serving by setting clear boundaries and being intentional about who and how he serves.

How do you build a company culture of compassion in a cutthroat industry? Check out Jonathan's book, *You Don't Have to Be Ruthless to*

Win, which outlines the fifteen principles for a selfless servant leadership culture at Keyser.[3]

Compassion Requires the Bravery to Be Vulnerable

One of the biggest challenges many leaders face when it comes to compassion is the vulnerability it takes to struggle with others. Leadership by its very nature can distance us from the day-to-day nitty-gritty work that generates the revenue. Dropping in to fix problems from a safe emotional distance is easy. Throwing money or resources at a problem is easy. Giving out advice day after day to employees who never seem to take ownership is draining but is still pretty easy compared to compassion.

What's missing in all these examples is the vulnerability that comes with sharing your struggles with another person. Helping another person from a safe place of authority or privilege still reinforces a sense of inequity. Most people find it much easier to help than to be helped, to alleviate suffering than to suffer alongside.

Compassion in leadership requires the vulnerability to open up your heart to another person. *You might not be equals on the organizational chart, but you are equals as humans. The only way to show that is to show your human side.* Research is full of evidence proving that leaders who show emotion, get real, and connect at a human level with their employees are more trusted and more effective.

Why then don't more leaders open up?

Massimo Backus is a certified professional coach and keynote speaker with expertise in organizational behavioral psychology, emotional intelligence, and team dynamics. He specializes in helping leaders practice self-compassion to regain their energy and enthusiasm and become a better leader.

Massimo learned this the hard way. He was the head of leadership development at a billion-dollar organization, and while outwardly successful at developing the people management and leadership skills of others in the organization, he himself was not behaving as a good leader of his own team. He was so focused on his expertise of developing others that he neglected to turn inward and focus on developing himself.

Think of it like this: he was a great basketball coach for his team, but he was not a great player on the court.

Massimo wasn't practicing what he preached. He had blind spots. He was missing so much of what was going on around him and inside him. He had good intentions and was trying desperately to keep up with his positive intentions, but his actions didn't follow.

The problem, Massimo explained, is that leaders believe all their experience, success, and titles should make them enough, yet they don't feel enough. Change starts inside with changing that identity and that means getting vulnerable. Leaders so often aren't comfortable with their own struggle, so they keep it hidden. If we can't be with ourselves in the challenges, how can we be with others in their struggles?

Amy Balog is an executive coach specializing in working with leaders who feel trapped in what she calls the "no-win, no-way-out purgatory of middle management." Middle managers, especially in large organizations, often feel helpless and exert so much energy trying to battle external factors over which they have no control. Amy calls this the *performance self*, a leader identity wrapped up in external performance that is never enough and is instead always searching.

The compassionate counterpart is what Amy calls the *peace self*, an identity based on unconditional value and self-acceptance. The peace self allows a leader to see more clearly, not be afraid of mistakes, separate their performance from their value, and stop trying to control things they can't. Here's how she describes the difference between the performance self and peace self: "Leaders try to perform in moments instead of knowing who they are and bringing themselves into the moment."[4] Bringing ourselves into the moment requires incredible bravery because it's vulnerable. The journey is difficult and scary, and it's worth it.

Many leaders we work with are terrified about the notion of being vulnerable, and for good reason. They haven't shown it before, so the experience is unknown. They worry that if they let themselves go there, they will never come out. They have experienced unhealthy examples of vulnerability. They see vulnerability as a liability because it's been abused. Most importantly, though, they simply don't know how to turn on their own value switch.

Getting vulnerable to struggle with others requires that leaders are emotionally aware and fluent. This alone can be a lifelong endeavor. Brené Brown, noted vulnerability researcher and author, reports that the average adult can identify and name three of their own emotions: happy, sad, and angry. In her book *Atlas of the Heart*, Brené describes eighty-seven human emotions and experiences.[5] That's a big gap between what we are aware of and what's actually there.

Atlas of the Heart is a remarkable road map for closing the gap. Brené has categorized emotions and experiences into relevant and intuitive chapters that capture the realities of what it means to be human in relationships. For example, the chapter titled "Places We Go with Others" covers the emotions and experiences of compassion, pity, empathy, sympathy, boundaries, and comparative suffering.

What I love about this book and why I recommend it to any leader who is trying to become more compassionate is how Brené covers each emotion and experience. First, she shares the research, explaining why we have it and what purpose it serves. Then, using poignant examples and personal stories, she explains how we can embrace our experience without judgment, articulate it to ourselves and others, and take responsibility for how we respond. *Atlas of the Heart* is a fantastic and effective road map for any leader who wants to begin the journey of emotional awareness and fluency, which some would call *self-compassion*. Being able to recognize, name, appreciate, articulate, and own the range of emotions we experience every day is critical for compassion with ourselves and others.

Even if you aren't ready to share your inner world with others, you can begin the journey of awareness to grow your emotional fluency.

Compassion Requires the Confidence to Be Humble

As if getting vulnerable weren't hard enough, compassion also requires self-confidence and humility, two qualities that can't exist without each other. Don't confuse humility with self-deprecation. Ken Blanchard, a bestselling author and top leadership expert on the topic of servant leadership, defines humility this way: *"Humility isn't thinking less of yourself. It's thinking of yourself less."*

Compassion definitely involves an aspect of helping, serving, and supporting others. How do we do that in the best way possible without unintended consequences? The story of my parents serving in Africa or David Katz's work with Plastic Bank would suggest that the most helpful acts are those that empower and build capability without compromising dignity and self-determination.

How do we ensure these outcomes? Without having the right mindset and motivation, most helping efforts will ultimately fail. The biggest threat to compassionate helping is ego. When we attempt to help others with the hidden motive of boosting our own ego, our effort is doomed from the start because drama is still present.

The following eight questions help you to determine if your helping behavior is serving your own ego and causing drama:

- Do you expect something in return?
- Do you help without being invited?
- Do you resent people who aren't grateful?
- Do you feel like a martyr?

- Do you find yourself in the line of fire, taking a bullet for some-one else?
- Do you keep a safe emotional distance?
- If it goes well, do you seek credit?
- If it goes bad, do you blame yourself or blame others?

All these signs have one thing in common. They all arise from the same false belief that our identity is dependent on the impact of our helping. This misunderstanding arises from lack of self-confidence.

Self-confidence means that we are comfortable in our skin and that we know our value as a human is secure and not conditional on external factors. When we let go of being defined by the impact of our efforts, then we can truly focus on the person we are struggling with. As Jonathan Keyser said, we can "fall in love with people" and focus on their best interests instead of our ego.[6] We can experience deep satisfaction in their success without needing credit. We can also partner with them along the way when things don't go well without interpreting set-backs as an indictment of who we are as human beings.

Compassion Requires the Courage to Walk the Talk

Jody Horner is the former president of Cargill Meat Solutions and Cargill Case Ready. In that role, she was responsible for a multibillion dollar corporation that supplied some of the world's largest retailers and led more than three thousand employees. During her term as pres-ident, Jody facilitated a high-growth strategy through approaches that increased employee engagement while dramatically reducing turnover at all levels.

Jody's story is a testament to how hard walking the talk is. I first met Jody in her home. She was on the board of Kansas Big Brothers Big Sisters at the time and was hosting a fundraising dinner. I was struck by her openness and warmth. I expected her to be tough-skinned and untouchable, especially given her role and the type of industry she was in. She doted over her French bulldog, loved talking about her children, and was transparent about their joys and struggles.

As I got to know Jody better and we became friends, I asked her about her experience as a female leader in such a male-dominated industry. She shared her story of rising through the ranks. She explained that what got people promoted was to be tough and show no weakness. She explained, "Basically, I learned to act like a jerk to get ahead." Over time, Jody realized that this mode wasn't authentic. It didn't feel right, nor was it consistent with who she was.

Jody knew she had to align her behavior with her true self, but she was afraid and anxious. She worried that her peers would lose respect for her and would see her as weak. But she took the risk to walk the talk. Motivated by her desire to make more meaningful, positive connections with people, Jody sought help from an executive coach. Soon she went from believing that she needed to make sure her armor had no chinks in it, being professional to a fault, to showing more of her real self at work, including telling people about her bulldog and her family.

What happened next was the exact opposite of what Jody feared most. She described it best: "My street credibility went through the roof." Jody experienced greater levels of trust and engagement in her team because they saw her as relatable. This created a turning point for her, a moment where she realized that vulnerability was her secret weapon and that walking the talk starts with being true to yourself and becoming a role model for what you value most.

Since leaving Cargill in 2009, Jody has returned to her roots and continued her love of education by serving as president of Midland University, a private university in Nebraska. Now her joy comes from building personal relationships with students, faculty, and constituency and creating a thriving and compassionate learning environment.

If They Can, So Can You

My parents became missionaries in their early twenties. They barely knew what they were doing and were scared to death. Bobby Herrera thought that leaders were supposed to be strong and hide their struggles. People thought Jonathan Keyser was crazy for serving others without expecting anything in return. Jody Horner worried that nobody would respect her if she let down her guard. But they all did it anyway. Because these people did the difficult and courageous work of walking the talk, they experienced and were able to practice compassion in a new and better way.

And so can you.

Main Points

- *The barrier*—When we view compassion as less relevant than other leadership skills or too soft to be taken seriously, we avoid doing the most important and difficult work of leadership.
- *The reality*—Compassion requires the bravery to be vulnerable, the confidence to be humble, and the courage to walk the talk. It's not soft or easy.
- *The hopeful message*—When leaders invest in personal transformation and authentic connection, it pays off many times over.
- *The lesson*—Accept that compassion is a necessary and relevant leadership skill, and approach it like any other core competency.
- *The leadership accountability*—You are accountable for developing your emotional awareness and fluency because they are fundamental leadership competencies.

CHAPTER 12

COMPASSION IS SELFLESS

"IF I GIVE, give, give all the time, won't I eventually burn out?"

"If I'm not 100 percent altruistic, will people question my integrity and sincerity?"

"How can I take care of myself while also serving others?"

Can you relate to any of these questions? If so, this chapter is for you.

Here's the reality and what this chapter is all about: *You are a valuable, capable, and responsible part of the compassion equation. You can and should take elegant care of yourself along the way. Plus, the personal benefits of compassion are tremendous.*

Being selfless can be interpreted in two different ways. One interpretation relates to humility, putting our ego aside so we can truly focus on what's best for others. This definition is the opposite of selfishness, and there's no problem with this. This aspect of compassion is important.

We can go too far with being selfless though. Problems arise when we show no regard for ourselves, putting ourselves last. A second interpretation of being selfless means leaving ourselves out of the equation.

Serving others at the expense of our own boundaries, health, and wellness is not sustainable and is a recipe for burnout.

To me, the biggest problem with this misconception is that it keeps us from taking elegant care of ourselves and experiencing and enjoying the personal benefits of compassion. If compassion is about struggling with others, then we must acknowledge that we are an important part of that equation. We should be at our best to fully embrace compassion. And it should be intrinsically rewarding. Both are okay.

Compassion Includes You and Invites You to Be Your Best

Everyone is valuable, capable, and responsible. That includes you. If you forget this, it will compromise your ability to help others. With the compassion mindset activated, here's how you fit in the equation.

Because you are valuable, you deserve to be heard, affirmed, safe, invited, and included. When you consider engaging with compassion, are you honoring these conditions with yourself? If you help someone in a way that compromises your safety, you aren't being compassionate with yourself. If you don't affirm your own feelings and needs and put them on the back burner so long that you begin to malfunction, that's not compassion. As a leader, if you compromise important boundaries and expectations to avoid difficult conversations, you send the message that you and the organization are less valuable than the person with whom you are having conflict. When you set boundaries, follow through, and take care of yourself, you send the message that everyone is equally valuable.

Because you are capable, you deserve to contribute, participate, take ownership, and be part of the solution. Struggling with is about working together toward something better. This involves contribution from both parties. How do you bring your best self into each relationship? How are you leveraging your strengths and experiences to support others?

Scott Shute is the former head of Mindfulness and Compassion Programs at LinkedIn. In this capacity, he led the development and implementation of initiatives to help employees practice more compassion with themselves and others. I asked Scott my usual question about compassion and selflessness. His belief is that we should follow our blisters, not our bliss.[1] There's a difference between what makes us happy and what we are continually drawn to. Our blisters might give us clues to where our purpose and passion really are.

When compassion is approached this way, we will likely serve until it hurts, but the effort has purpose and connects us to our deepest joy. In fact, it connects us more fully to who we are rather than inviting us to leave ourselves behind. It hurts so good.

Because you are responsible, you are accountable for your feelings, thoughts, and actions. It's relatively common to talk about being responsible for your actions since these behaviors are most visible. But what about feelings and thoughts? In the previous chapter, I talked about emotional fluency, which is a fundamental component of being responsible. Each of us is responsible for our emotions. Nobody caused them, and you can't export them to someone else. Yet every day, we act as if something or someone is responsible for our feelings. We say, "He made me so mad," "That really triggered me," or "How did it make you feel when she stood you up?" These behaviors are emotionally irresponsible. They seek to blame someone else for our emotions rather than taking responsibility for them.

Life happens. We can't control much of what happens to us. What occurs next, however, is our responsibility. What does it look like to take responsibility for your emotions? It means understanding that emotions are a product of combining what happens to us with the story we tell ourselves about it. Owning your emotions means being able to identify and name them and articulate the story you tell yourself. Two people can have the same thing happen to them, but have different emotions. That's because they have distinct experiences, coping mechanisms, and stories. Our stories are influenced by our history, personality, and values and a host of other factors that are unique to us. While you might not like what happened to you or how someone treated you, your emotions and the story you tell yourself about it are uniquely yours. You are responsible for what you do next.

If we don't take responsibility for our feelings and thoughts, then we can get confused about who's responsible for our behavior. If I falsely believe that "you disrespected me by being late," then I can justify my passive-aggressive behavior later at dinner. If I falsely believe that you can make me feel bad by rejecting me, then I might go overboard trying to please you and avoid setting boundaries for fear of making you mad. Feel free to review chapter 6 for more examples.

Compassion requires that we take 100 percent responsibility for our feelings, thoughts, and behaviors. Otherwise our relationships can easily become one-sided, self-serving, or harmful. As a leader, you are always training people on how to treat you.

When you give in, give a pass, or give preferential treatment, you are sending the message that not everyone is equally valuable, capable, or responsible. This behavior is not compassionate, and it doesn't represent you at your best.

Compassion Is Intrinsically Rewarding

Silvia Garcia is the former global marketing director for Coca-Cola and was the director for Coca-Cola's happiness institute. She spent a good portion of her career studying the effects of compassion and kindness. She shared with me that the most consistent finding, which held true in every country and culture, was that acts of kindness benefit the giver more than the receiver. Silvia's research showed that while the recipients of acts of kindness certainly benefited, those who initiated them experienced the biggest gains in happiness and physical well-being.[2]

Laurel Donnellan writes a column for *Forbes* magazine featuring leaders who epitomize compassion in their lives and sponsors an annual compassionate leader award. Laurel is dedicated to lifting up and learning from compassionate leaders. She shared with me that she has discovered over and over with her guests and in her own life that *"Compassion is for the giver as well as the receiver. I get ten times the enjoyment back when I give to others."*[3]

Brain science supports the intrinsic, positive impact of compassion. Neurobiological research reported by Drs. Stephen Trzeciak and Anthony Mazzarelli in their book, *Compassionomics*, shows that compassion, defined as actively engaging with someone to help, triggers the reward centers of the brain.[4] Compassion has an effect on the body that is nourishing. It lights up the love regions of the brain. It causes a release of oxytocin, which then causes a release of dopamine and serotonin. The result is feelings of pleasure, joy, and reduced anxiety.

In comparison, empathy activates the pain centers of the brain. When we feel someone's pain, we really feel it. This biological reaction is why empathy alone, without active engagement to struggle with others toward a solution, can be so draining. Empathy fatigue is a real phenomenon and can lead to burnout.[5]

When I spoke with Stephen, I asked him about what can be done to help reverse the crisis of burnout among medical providers. He emphasized how important it is to distinguish empathy from compassion and shared some hopeful research. Physicians who are taught basic strategies to engage with compassion can regain their energy and passion. Contrary to the distancing and depersonalization often associated with burnout, when healthcare professionals lean into the patient relationship in a more collaborative way, they experience more energy, purpose, and satisfaction. Stephen suggests that this research translates far beyond healthcare settings and should give hope to any leader who experiences empathy fatigue or avoids engaging at a personal level because they fear the emotional drain.

Leaning in with compassion is more healthy than checking out.

Our research supports Stephen's prediction. Fifteen years of outcomes research shows that when we teach leaders how to engage with compassion, they experience increases in self-efficacy, a greater sense of leadership effectiveness, and more trust among their teams. One of the biggest benefits is reversing the energy drain of drama. Compassion is the antidote to drama.[6]

If you've been conditioned to give until it hurts, you might be a candidate for burnout. But if you can embrace the intrinsic restorative benefits of compassion, think of how much better your life could be. Imagine the possibilities if you practiced a kind of compassion that leaves you more energized at the end of the day.

Compassion Is Self-ful

Being self-ful isn't the same as being selfish. Being self-ful means putting your oxygen mask on before attempting to help the person in the seat next to you. It means taking responsibility for filling your tank and charging your battery every day so that you can serve others and do so without guilt. It means taking 100 percent responsibility for your feelings, thoughts, and actions.

Dan Rockwell is an executive coach and is known as the Leadership Freak. He has one of the most read blogs in the industry and is an expert in what it means to be a compassionate leader. When I asked him about being self-ful, he summed it up this way: *"If you want to pour a lot out of your life, pour a lot in."*[7]

From her home in Taiwan, Jill Chang oversees the operations of more than twenty countries for Give2Asia, an international philanthropy advisory firm based in San Francisco. She has delivered over two hundred speeches and training sessions in different countries and was the winner of Girls in Tech Taiwan 40 under 40 in 2018. Jill is also an extreme introvert and is on a mission to help introverts succeed in the workplace just as she has. Her book, *Quiet Is a Superpower*, was a bestseller in Taiwan, the United States, and Japan. She is often referred to as "Taiwan's Susan Cain."[8]

Jill couldn't survive and thrive like she does without being self-ful. For her, taking good care of herself is all about energy management. Jill explains that energy is her most precious asset, and how she manages it determines whether she can deliver on her obligations and be present with the most important people and projects in her life. To manage her energy requires careful planning, setting boundaries, and taking time alone to recharge every day. What does energy management mean for you?

Gloria Cotton is one of the kindest and most loving, strong, and convicted people you will ever meet. She's a senior partner at inQuest Consulting, a collective of DEI thought leaders with years of experience working with clients in complex, dynamic environments. She's been studying, training, and speaking about DEI for many years and realizes the importance of having compassion for yourself first in this line of work.

I spoke with Gloria about what being self-ful means when you are working day after day in situations that are unjust, unfair, and inequitable. For Gloria, it came to a head after George Floyd, a Black man, was murdered by a white police officer in Minneapolis in 2020. Normally pretty good at managing her emotions, Gloria shared how her response to this event really took her by surprise.[9] The depth and strength and darkness of her reactions was almost overwhelming. What she realized during this was that to engage compassionately with others, you first have to be an ally to yourself. She had to show self-compassion to talk herself off the cliff. Her advice to anyone doing difficult emotional work was "Don't deny or judge your own feelings. Make peace with what's going on within you before you respond to the warring outside of you."

Compassion is hard work. Being a compassionate leader means we will confront conflict, suffering, and injustice. Without taking elegant care of ourselves, we won't last long. Being self-ful is fundamental to a fuller understanding and practice of compassion.

Main Points

- *The barrier*—If compassion means putting ourselves last, we won't be able to sustain the difficult work, and we won't experience the intrinsic satisfaction that comes with it.
- *The reality*—You are a valuable, capable, and responsible part of the compassion equation. You can and should take elegant care of yourself along the way.
- *The hopeful message*—When you become self-ful as a leader, you can experience the intrinsic, restorative benefits of compassion for yourself.
- *The lesson*—Take 100 percent responsibility for your feelings, thoughts, and actions. This means being self-ful so you can show up with the energy and enthusiasm to face the difficult challenges of being a leader.
- *The leadership accountability*—You are accountable for your feelings, thoughts, and actions. This means you can't blame others for your experiences, and you can't take over responsibility for others' feelings, thoughts, and actions. You are accountable to stay on the right side of that fine line. When you do, others will be invited and inspired to do the same.

CHAPTER 13

COMPASSION CAN'T
BE LEARNED

"ISN'T COMPASSION something you are born with and just comes naturally for some people?"

"If I'm not good at it, won't people question my motives?"

"I didn't learn how to be compassionate growing up. Is it too late?"

Can you relate to any of these questions? If so, this chapter is for you.

Here's the reality and what this chapter is all about: *compassion, like any other leadership competency, can be learned.*

"Some people just have it" is a popular barrier to avoid changing behavior. Many believe compassion is some kind of inborn, natural capability that some people have and some don't. This idea is not only a barrier but also a convenient excuse. If a task is hard for me or I make a mistake, I can make the excuse that I just don't have it in me. Conversely, if I'm good at it, I can easily forget the hard work and practice I put in to do it well. Here are a few other versions of this excuse:

- "You're a natural. You make it look so easy."
- "I'm too old and set in my ways."
- "It doesn't feel authentic."
- "I don't have time."
- "I'll probably just make the situation worse if I don't do it right."
- "Compassion is for big-hearted people. That's not me."

The problem with this misconception is that it lowers self-confidence and holds people back from developing their compassion skills.

Compassion Can Be Learned

A Harvard study showed that 56 percent of physicians believe they don't have time to treat patients with compassion.[1] Yet the evidence is clear that it takes less than a minute. Or if you replace brusque business behaviors with compassion, you can experience a net gain. Researchers from Johns Hopkins University tested the impact of an enhanced compassion intervention for cancer patients to see if it could impact patient anxiety.[2] The intervention was simple. They would start each consultation with this message:

> I know this is a tough experience to go through, and I want you to know that I am here with you. Some of the things that I say to you today may be difficult to understand, so I want you to feel comfortable in stopping me if something I say is confusing or doesn't make sense. We are here together, and we will go through this together.

At the end of the consultation, the oncologist finished with this:

> I know this is a tough time for you, and I want to emphasize again that we are in this together. I will be with you each step of the way.

How long did that take? Just forty seconds. and it resulted in statistically significant reductions in patient anxiety and a greater sense of satisfaction in physicians that they had made a meaningful impact.

Beyond scripting interventions for doctors, compassion can be learned at a deeper level as well.

We teach compassion principles and strategies every day to leaders, and we measure the results. Most of our clients are trying to bring more Compassionate Accountability into their daily interactions, particularly around difficult conversations, conflict, and other situations with a high potential for drama. We teach specific strategies and a template for conducting these conversations, much like what the oncologists were given in the Johns Hopkins study. However, our training is a bit more sophisticated because leaders need adaptive templates and strategies that they can apply across a broad range of interactions on the fly to guide difficult interactions beyond the first statement. Within several training sessions, along with coached feedback, our clients are able to implement these strategies in their flow of work and begin to see positive results in the form of more positive interactions, less drama, and quicker resolution of issues.

At a macro level, we track changes in self-efficacy, a person's confidence in their ability to apply new behaviors to meet particular challenges. Specifically, we measure changes in a person's confidence in their ability to be open, resourceful, and persistent—three critical components of Compassionate Accountability.

Openness is the ability to show confident transparency, connect with others in an emotional way, and create psychological safety. Resourcefulness is the ability to apply creative problem-solving and engage others in collaboration. Persistence is about staying the course and adhering to principles and commitments. These critical leadership competencies create safe, curious, and consistent work cultures.

Often we ask participants to assess their efficacy in multiple contexts so we can see the differential impact of their efforts at home, at work, or in their team. Table 13.1 shows data collected across all our programs over the past decade. Change is expressed in terms of effect size, which demonstrates the direction and magnitude of change.

Here's a review of how to interpret effect sizes, as shown in table 13.1. An effect size measures the magnitude of change in a group of scores, expressed in terms of standard deviation units. In other words, how much did the average self-efficacy score improve? An effect size of 0.25 means that the average score increased by 0.25 standard deviations. This is considered educationally significant—that is, people learned something. Effect sizes of 0.50 are considered clinically significant, meaning a deeper level of transformation.

Table 13.1 shows that on average, Compassionate Accountability training results in changes that are beyond educationally significant. The strongest impact is in the area of "Openness at work" (0.38 effect size). These results are encouraging because the research is clear that openness and vulnerability is the biggest predictor of leadership success and is the least developed of the three areas among the leaders we work with. Making a greater impact in this domain of compassion is what we want. Our training and coaching work focuses heavily on developing leadership openness.

We also assess impact in relevant areas of a leader's life. All participants in our programs are asked to assess the percent improvement in

TABLE 13.1. Effect sizes for changes in self-efficacy

	Openness	Resourcefulness	Persistence
Me at home	.31	.28	.32
Me at work	.38	.31	.31
My team	.31	.26	.28

TABLE 13.2. Percentage change in four areas of focus that participants attribute to Compassionate Accountability training

Area of impact	Percent improvement attributed to Compassionate Accountability training
Personal relationships	69 percent
Work relationships	71 percent
Leadership skills	70 percent
Teamwork	72 percent

four areas, which they would attribute to the training. Table 13.2 shows our twelve-year cumulative results.

Table 13.2's data suggests strong positive changes in relevant areas of a leader's life attributable to their efforts to learn and implement more compassion.

For the research purists, I recognize that our outcomes research isn't up to the highest academic standards. The messy nature of collecting outcomes and impact data means we don't conduct randomized controlled studies, and we don't always measure all four of James Kirkpatrick's levels of training evaluation: reaction, learning, behavior, and results.[3] However, our data does suggest that behavior is changing and impacting the outcomes that matter to the leaders and their organizations.

How Does Change Happen?

Tom Kolditz is an internationally recognized expert on crisis leadership and leadership in extreme contexts and the founding director of the Doerr Institute for New Leaders at Rice University. The Doerr Institute was recognized in 2019 as the top university leader development program by the Association of Leadership Educators and named the fourth best leadership development program in the world by Global Gurus.

Tom is leading a movement to increase rigor and integrity around leadership training at the university level. He's a retired brigadier general, taught leadership at West Point for twelve years, and is a researcher by training. He has no room for investing time and energy into leadership training that doesn't work, so the Doerr Institute is obsessive about research.

I talked to Tom about leader development at Doerr and the research outlined in his book *Leadership Reckoning*.[4] He described how they have identified best practices for leader development based on research showing that new behavioral skills can be learned and that certain factors predict leader success more than others. In particular, the most important factors predicting students' success as leaders have to do with their own identity and desire for leadership and their social-emotional skills.

We've seen a similar phenomenon in our work, one that's probably familiar to anyone in the learning and development field. Every group of learners is made up of three subgroups. One group, which we call the lifelong learners, enthusiastically embraces the opportunity to learn and grow and takes full advantage of the opportunity. They are coachable and curious and not afraid to make mistakes. Consequently, they excel and experience benefits in their life.

A second group we call cautious skeptics. They don't warm up easily and need time to discern if their efforts are worth their investment. This group can jump on board and become the most loyal and hardest working group if treated with respect and patience. Or they can dig in their heels and refuse to engage if rushed or pressured.

A third group can be a single individual, but they are almost always present. We call them the saboteurs. These people actively attempt to sabotage the process, usually because they feel threatened by it. If the training process proceeds as it should with support from top leadership, these people usually get fired or choose to leave because they see change happening in a direction they don't want to go. Once in a great while, they experience a transformation. The worst outcome is when they aren't held accountable and the organization is exposed as not having the courage to walk the talk.

I've seen this phenomena my whole life, in all sorts of settings, even as a psychologist leading inpatient addiction recovery groups. I view this as a challenge. How can I engage the unengaged, turn sabotage into participation, and persuade people to embrace their own potential for positive change? If you share my passion, you've probably also realized that a trainer, coach, teacher, or consultant can do only so much. That's because a lot of it depends on the learner and what they bring to the party.

As a student of human change, I am always curious as to why people do what they do and how we can use that information to improve positive impact. In our quest to uncover the secret, we asked ourselves, Why do some people seem to take off when presented with an opportunity to learn and grow while others stay stuck? We started looking for clues during our training programs. Right away we discovered several factors that didn't matter, including intelligence or effort. Everyone in our programs is smart and motivated. Most exert effort; only some thrive. The others continually hit barriers or put up walls. Why?

In 2019 we discovered the answer, and it didn't surprise us.

The Power of Mindset

We discovered that the difference between leaders who fly and leaders who stay on the ground is mindset. What makes all the difference is how they view themselves and others. We began to observe the mindset at play in how they approached learning, handled mistakes, and reacted to each other along the way. When we began to map the mindset, we discovered that it paralleled almost exactly what we were teaching as the fundamental compassion skills. In other words, a compassion mindset is the foundation for learning and practicing compassion.

The beauty of a mindset is that we can change it. A mindset is a choice, attitude, and way of thinking that can change behavior and be reinforced through behavior. Carol Dweck is the researcher who made famous the notion of mindset by demonstrating how success in school, work, sports, the arts, and almost every area of human endeavor can be dramatically influenced by how we think about our talents and abilities. People with a fixed mindset—those who believe that abilities are fixed—are less likely to flourish than those with a growth mindset—those who believe that abilities can be developed.[5] A growth mindset aligns most closely with the capability switch of the compassion mindset.

So the compassion mindset is more comprehensive and applies to the practice of Compassionate Accountability. As you know from reading this book, the compassion mindset is a framework for how leaders and organizations can build their cultures of Compassionate Accountability.

Main Points

- *The barrier*—If we believe that some people are just more compassionate by nature, this lowers self-confidence and holds us back from developing our compassion skills.
- *The reality*—Compassion, like any other leadership competency, can be learned.
- *The hopeful message*—Leaders no longer have to make excuses. They can be confident that their efforts will pay off.

- *The lesson*—Mindset matters. Instead of making excuses or losing confidence, make the choice to change your mindset. This will open up new possibilities for you to learn and grow.
- *The leadership accountability*—You are accountable for your mindset. Every day in every interaction, you get to choose how you will view yourself and others and how you will show up as a leader.

APPENDIX

THE COMPASSIONATE ACCOUNTABILITY ASSESSMENT

WHETHER YOU are trying to improve yourself, your team, or your entire organization, an honest assessment is critical. Use the Compassionate Accountability Assessment below to assess how often the target behaviors for each switch are being demonstrated. You can also download a digital copy of this assessment by visiting Compassionate AccountabilityBook.com.

There are no right or wrong answers. However, by scoring yourself, your team, and your organization on the three switches, you will be able to see where your strengths and weaknesses are and set goals for improvement.

For each target behavior, rate how often you experience this in yourself, your team, and your organization in tables A.1, A.2, and A.3.

Once you've calculated the averages for each switch, copy them into table A.4.

TABLE A.1. Value

Value switch target behavior 0 = never 1 = seldom 2 = occasionally 3 = frequently	Myself	My team	My organiza-tion
Listens to and validates feelings without judging	_____	_____	_____
Assumes positive intentions and checks assumptions	_____	_____	_____
Affirms experiences, even if I or others can't relate to them	_____	_____	_____
Empathizes by finding common emotional ground	_____	_____	_____
Is transparent by sharing own feelings, motives, and experiences	_____	_____	_____
Is willing to be vulnerable	_____	_____	_____
Demonstrates that you don't have to agree with someone to value them as a person	_____	_____	_____
Separates the person from the behavior	_____	_____	_____
Includes and leverages diversity	_____	_____	_____
Value totals: Add up totals for each column	_____	_____	_____
Value averages: Divide total by 9 to obtain average for each category	_____	_____	_____

TABLE A.2. Capability

Capability switch target behavior 0 = never 1 = seldom 2 = occasionally 3 = frequently	Myself	My team	My organiza-tion
Seeks first to understand	____	____	____
Shares ideas and resources to find the best solutions	____	____	____
Invites people to be part of the solution	____	____	____
Invests in others' successes	____	____	____
Turns failure into learning opportunities	____	____	____
Capability totals: Add up totals for each column	____	____	____
Capability averages: Divide total by 5 to obtain average for each category	____	____	____

TABLE A.3. Responsibility

Responsibility switch target behavior 0 = never 1 = seldom 2 = occasionally 3 = frequently	Myself	My team	My organization
Takes ownership over own emotions, thoughts, and behaviors	——	——	——
Allows others to take ownership over their emotions, thoughts, and behaviors	——	——	——
Asks directly and assertively for what is wanted and needed	——	——	——
Enforces boundaries, standards, and commitments without blaming, attacking, or threatening	——	——	——
Keeps the most important thing the most important thing	——	——	——
Responsibility totals: Add up totals for each column	——	——	——
Responsibility averages: Divide total by 5 to obtain average for each category	——	——	——

TABLE A.4. Compassion mindset switch averages

Compassion mindset switch averages	Myself	My team	My organization
Value	_____	_____	_____
Capability	_____	_____	_____
Responsibility	_____	_____	_____
Compassionate accountability score: Average the scores for each switch	_____	_____	_____

Plotting Your Scores

Using figures A.1, A.2, and A.3, plot your scores for each switch. You can also download a digital copy of this assessment by visiting CompassionateAccountabilityBook.com.

Interpreting Your Scores

The lower the score, the more risk for toxic cultures with low engagement, high turnover, and failure to perform. The higher the score, the more potential for thriving cultures with high engagement, low turnover, and capacity to perform. Use figures A.1, A.2, and A.3 to track your scores.

0–1 = Danger zone—Compassionate Accountability is lacking. Make changes immediately.

1–2 = Potential zone—Pockets of Compassionate Accountability are present. Nurture them.

2–2.5 = Opportunity zone—Compassionate Accountability is taking hold. Build momentum.

2.5–3 = Strength zone—Compassionate Accountability is alive and active. Keep it up!

Remember that each switch is necessary but not sufficient on its own for Compassionate Accountability to work. If all three switches in a particular domain (self, team, or organization) have a score above 2, Compassionate Accountability is taking hold. If any of the three switches are under 2, this represents an area of potential for growth.

Continue to interpret and apply your Compassionate Accountability Assessment results using the guidance in chapter 7.

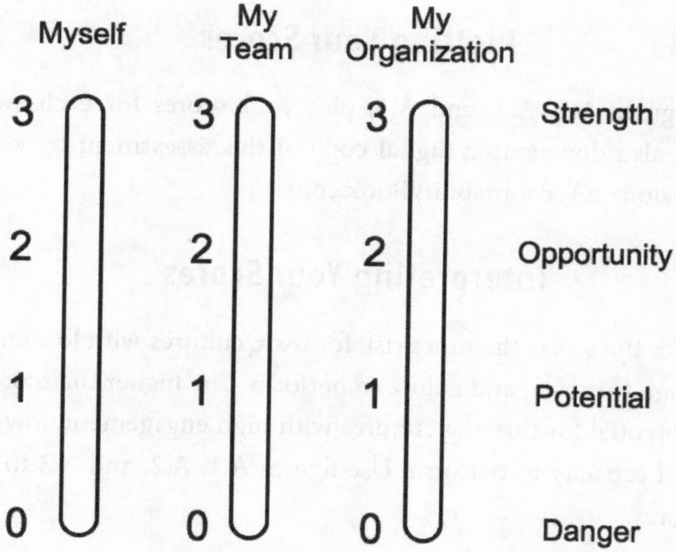

FIGURE A.1. Value switch scoring template.
Designed by Nate Regier.

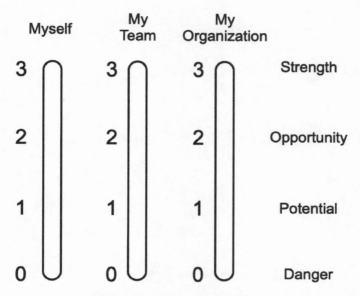

FIGURE A.2. Capability switch scoring template.
Designed by Nate Regier.

Myself	My Team	My Organization	
3	3	3	Strength
2	2	2	Opportunity
1	1	1	Potential
0	0	0	Danger

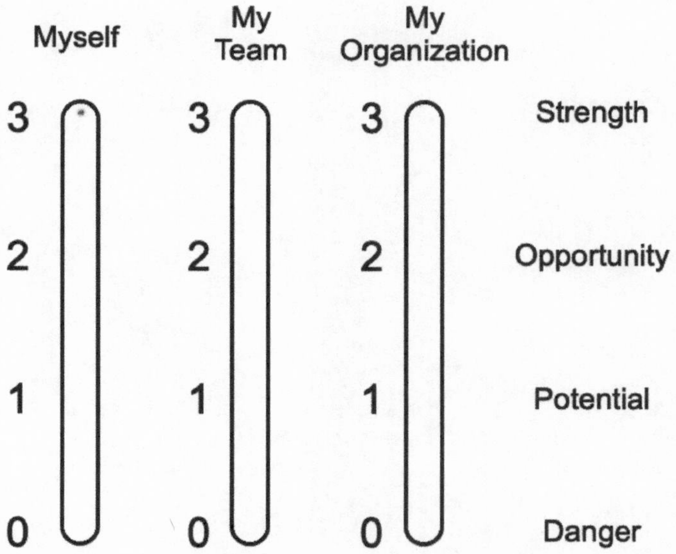

FIGURE A.3. Responsibility switch scoring template.
Designed by Nate Regier.

FIGURE 2: ... style ... designed by ...

FIGURE 3: ... designed by ...

NOTES

Chapter 1

1. Myers Briggs Company, "New Study Details Both Crippling and Beneficial Effects of Workplace Conflict on Businesses," press release, October 6, 2008, shop.themyersbriggs.com/PRESS/Workplace_Conflict_Study.aspx.

2. Donald Sull, Charles Sull, and Ben Zweig, "Toxic Culture Is Driving the Great Resignation," *MIT Sloan Management Review*, January 11, 2022, sloanreview.mit.edu/article/toxic-culture-is-driving-the-great-resignation/.

3. Blaine Bartlett and David Meltzer, *Compassionate Capitalism: Journey to the Soul of Business* (Pasadena, CA: Best Seller Publishing, 2016).

4. Monica Worline and Jane Dutton, *Awakening Compassion at Work: The Quiet Power That Elevates People and Organizations* (Oakland, CA: Berrett-Koehler, 2017).

5. Rasmus Hougaard, Jacqueline Carter, and Nick Hobson, "Compassionate Leadership Is Necessary—but Not Sufficient," *Harvard Business Review*, December 4, 2020, hbr.org/2020/12/compassionate-leadership-is-necessary-but-not-sufficient.

6. Lucy Leclerc et al., "Relational Leadership: A Contemporary, Evidence-Based Approach to Improving Nursing Work Environments," *Nursing Management* 53, no. 7 (July 2022): 24–34.

7. Larry Kim, "The Results of Google's Team-Effectiveness Research Will Make You Rethink How You Build Teams," Medium, December 26, 2017, medium.com/the-mission/the-results-of-googles-team-effectiveness-research-will-make-you-rethink-how-you-build-teams-902aa61b33.

8. Scott Shute, *The Full Body Yes: Change Your Work and Your World from the Inside Out* (Vancouver, BC: Page Two Books, 2021).

9. Gloria Cotton, "Being a Pro-Inclusionist" (presentation, Association for Learning Providers, Annual Business Retreat, Scottsdale, AZ, March 28, 2022).

10. Tom Henry, "Conscious Capitalism with Tom Henry," interview by Nate Regier, in *On Compassion with Dr. Nate*, podcast, March 30, 2020, oncompassion.libsyn.com/conscious-capitalism-with-tom-henry.

11. Garry Ridge and Martha Finney, *The Unexpected Learning Moment: Lessons in Leading a Thriving Culture through Lockdown 2020* (Dublin, OH: Telemachus Press, 2021).

12. Rob McKenna, "Investing in the Whole Person as a Leader with Rob McKenna," interview by Nate Regier, in *On Compassion with Dr. Nate*, podcast, August 1, 2022, oncompassion.libsyn.com/investing-in-the-whole -person-as-a-leader-with-rob-mckenna.

Chapter 2

1. Rob McKenna, *Composed: The Heart and Science of Leading under Pressure* (Oklahoma City: Dust Jacket Press, 2017).

2. Doug Conant, "An Approachable Model for Leadership with Doug Conant," interview by Nate Regier, in *On Compassion with Dr. Nate*, podcast, September 2, 2019, oncompassion.libsyn.com/an-approachable-model-for -leadership-with-doug-conant.

3. Conant, "An Approachable Model."

4. Conant, "An Approachable Model."

5. Douglas Conant and Mette Norgaard, *TouchPoints: Creating Powerful Leadership Connections in the Smallest of Moments* (San Francisco: Jossey-Bass, 2011).

6. Wikipedia, s.v. "Peter Principle," last modified January 16, 2023, en.wikipedia.org/wiki/Peter_principle.

7. Ken Blanchard and Randy Conley, *Simple Truths of Leadership: 52 Ways to Be a Servant Leader and Build Trust* (Oakland, CA: Berrett-Koehler, 2022).

Chapter 4

1. Rob McKenna, "Investing in the Whole Person as a Leader with Rob McKenna," interview by Nate Regier, in *On Compassion with Dr. Nate*, podcast, August 1, 2022, oncompassion.libsyn.com/investing-in-the-whole -person-as-a-leader-with-rob-mckenna.

2. Tom Henry, "Conscious Capitalism with Tom Henry," interview by Nate Regier, in *On Compassion with Dr. Nate*, podcast, March 30, 2020, oncompassion.libsyn.com/conscious-capitalism-with-tom-henry.

3. Marcus Engle, *I'm Here: Compassionate Communication in Patient Care*, 3rd ed. (Orlando, FL: Phillips Press, 2010).

4. Gloria Cotton, "Being a Pro-Inclusionist" (presentation, Association for Learning Providers, Annual Business Retreat, Scottsdale, AZ, March 28, 2022).

5. Garry Ridge, "Create a Culture: Belong to a Tribe (Not a Team) with Garry Ridge," interview by Nate Regier, in *On Compassion with Dr. Nate*, podcast, December 1, 2021, oncompassion.libsyn.com/create-a-culture -belong-to-a-tribe-not-a-team-with-gary-ridge.

6. Bobby Herrera, *The Gift of Struggle: Life-Changing Lessons about Leading* (Austin, TX: Bard Press, 2019).

7. Arbinger Institute, *The Anatomy of Peace: Resolving the Heart of Conflict* (Oakland, CA: Berrett-Koehler, 2015).

8. Marlene Chism, *From Conflict to Courage: How to Stop Avoiding and Start Leading* (Oakland, CA: Berrett-Koehler, 2022).

9. Marlene Chism, "Do Conflict in a Healthy Way with Marlene Chism," interview by Nate Regier, in *On Compassion with Dr. Nate*, podcast, October 1, 2022, oncompassion.libsyn.com/do-conflict-in-a-healthy-way-with -marlene-chism.

10. Adam Grant (@AdamMGrant), "Vulnerability is not the opposite of resilience. Vulnerability builds resilience. Projecting perfection protects your ego but shuts people out and stunts your growth," Twitter, February 24, 2021, 12:15 p.m., twitter.com/AdamMGrant/status/136467026248 2993154.

11. Amy Balog, "Escaping the Purgatory of Middle Management with Amy Balog," interview by Nate Regier, in *On Compassion with Dr. Nate*, podcast, November 1, 2022, oncompassion.libsyn.com/the-middle -managers-struggle-feeling-stuck-and-overloaded-with-amy-balog.

12. Nate Regier, "I Appreciate You vs. I Appreciate It," Next Element (blog), October 28, 2020, next-element.com/resources/blog/appreciate -you-vs-appreciate-it/.

Chapter 5

1. Liz Wiseman with Greg McKeown, *Multipliers: How the Best Managers Make Everyone Smarter* (New York: Harper Business, 2017).

2. Marlene Chism, "Do Conflict in a Healthy Way with Marlene Chism," interview by Nate Regier, in *On Compassion with Dr. Nate*, podcast, October 1, 2022, oncompassion.libsyn.com/do-conflict-in-a-healthy-way-with -marlene-chism.

3. Karin Hurt and David Dye, *Courageous Cultures: How to Build Teams of Microinnovators, Problem-Solvers, and Customer Advocates* (New York: HarperCollins Leadership, 2020).

4. Garry Ridge, "Create a Culture: Belong to a Tribe (Not a Team) with Garry Ridge," interview by Nate Regier, in *On Compassion with Dr. Nate*, podcast, December 1, 2021, oncompassion.libsyn.com/create-a-culture -belong-to-a-tribe-not-a-team-with-gary-ridge.

5. Blaine Bartlett and David Meltzer, *Compassionate Capitalism: Journey to the Soul of Business* (Pasadena, CA: Best Seller Publishing, 2016).

6. Larry Carlson, "Self-Care and Compassion with HBO's Renaissance Man Larry Carlson," interview by Nate Regier, in *On Compassion with Dr. Nate*, podcast, December 1, 2020, oncompassion.libsyn.com/compassion -with-hbos-renaissance-man-larry-carlson.

7. Wikipedia, s.v. "Self-Efficacy," last modified January 2, 2023, en.wikipedia.org/wiki/Self-efficacy.

Chapter 6

1. Nate Regier, *Conflict without Casualties: A Field Guide for Leading with Compassionate Accountability* (Oakland, CA: Berrett-Koehler, 2017).

2. Scott Shute, *The Full Body Yes: Change Your Work and Your World from the Inside Out* (Vancouver, BC: Page Two Books, 2021).

3. Ken Blanchard and Randy Conley, "Servant Leadership, Trust, and Compassion with Ken Blanchard and Randy Conley," interview by Nate Regier, in *On Compassion with Dr. Nate*, podcast, June 1, 2022, oncompassion.libsyn.com/servant-leadership-trust-and-compassion-with-ken-blanchard-and-randy-conley.

4. Ken Blanchard and Randy Conley, *Simple Truths of Leadership: 52 Ways to Be a Servant Leader and Build Trust* (Oakland, CA: Berrett-Koehler, 2022).

5. Marlene Chism, *From Conflict to Courage: How to Stop Avoiding and Start Leading* (Oakland, CA: Berrett-Koehler, 2022).

6. Laura Cole, "Leadership, Conflict and Compassion with Laura Cole," interview by Nate Regier, in *On Compassion with Dr. Nate*, podcast, September 2, 2019, oncompassion.libsyn.com/leadership-conflict-and-compassion-with-laura-cole.

7. Jarrod Davis, "Values vs. Beliefs," Barrett Values Centre (blog), May 29, 2022, valuescentre.com/values-vs-beliefs/.

8. Tom Henry, "Conscious Capitalism with Tom Henry," interview by Nate Regier, in *On Compassion with Dr. Nate*, podcast, March 30, 2020, oncompassion.libsyn.com/conscious-capitalism-with-tom-henry.

9. Nate Regier, "How to Make a Better Apology: Round 2 with Nate's Podcast," Next Element (blog), June 13, 2017, next-element.com/resources/blog/four-simple-steps-to-make-a-better-apology/.

Chapter 7

1. Mark C. Crowley, *Lead from the Heart: Transformational Leadership for the 21st Century*, 2nd ed. (Carlsbad, CA: Hay House, 2022).

2. Seth Godin, "People Like Us Do Things Like This," *Seth's Blog*, July 23, 2013, seths.blog/2013/07/people-like-us-do-stuff-like-this/.

Chapter 9

1. Lea Winerman, "The Mind's Mirror," *Monitor*, American Psychological Association, October 2005, apa.org/monitor/oct05/mirror.

2. Nate Regier, *Seeing People Through: Unleash Your Leadership Potential with the Process Communication Model* (Oakland, CA: Berrett-Koehler, 2020).

3. "Process Communication Model (PCM)," Next Element, next -element.com/resources/compassion-accountability-tools/pcm.

4. Nate Regier, "The Six Love Handles of Communication," Next Element (blog), September 15, 2021, next-element.com/resources/blog /the-six-love-handles-of-communication.

5. Tahira Reid Smith, "Compassion Meets Engineering Design with Dr. Tahira Reid Smith," interview by Nate Regier, in *On Compassion with Dr. Nate*, podcast, October 1, 2021, oncompassion.libsyn.com -compassion-meets-engineering-design-with-dr-tahira-reid-smith.

6. Kristen Donelly, "Empathy and Compassion Are Daily Practices with Kristen Donelly," interview by Nate Regier, in *On Compassion with Dr. Nate*, podcast, April 1, 2022, oncompassion.libsyn.com/empathy-and -compassion-are-daily-practices-with-kristen-donelly.

Chapter 10

1. Laurel Donnellan, "Compassionate Leaders with Laurel Donnellan," interview by Nate Regier, in *On Compassion with Dr. Nate*, podcast, September 1, 2020, oncompassion.libsyn.com/compassionate-leaders -with-laurel-donnellan.

2. Nate Regier, "Ten Permissions That Should Be Part of Every Leadership Training Program," Next Element (blog), April 14, 2021, next -element.com/resources/blog/ten-permissions-that-will-add-positive -energy-to-your-life.

3. Wikipedia, s.v. "Karpman Drama Triangle," last modified December 23, 2022, en.wikipedia.org/wiki/Karpman_drama_triangle.

4. "Burn-Out an 'Occupational Phenomenon': International Classification of Diseases," World Health Organization, May 28, 2019,

who.int/news/item/28-05-2019-burn-out-an-occupational-phenomenon
-international-classification-of-diseases.

5. Ashley Abramson, "Burnout and Stress Are Everywhere," *Monitor*,
American Psychological Association, January 1, 2022, apa.org/monitor
/2022/01/special-burnout-stress.

6. "Employee Burnout Is Ubiquitous, Alarming—and Still
Underreported," McKinsey & Company, April 16, 2021, mckinsey.com
/featured-insights/coronavirus-leading-through-the-crisis/charting-the
-path-to-the-next-normal/employee-burnout-is-ubiquitous-alarming-and
-still-underreported.

7. National Academy of Medicine, *Taking Action against Clinician
Burnout: A Systems Approach to Professional Well-Being*, October 2019,
nam.edu/wp-content/uploads/2019/10/CR-report-highlights-brief-final
.pdf.

8. Stephen Trzeciak and Anthony Mazzarelli, *Compassionomics: The
Revolutionary Scientific Evidence That Caring Makes a Difference* (Pensacola,
FL: Studer Group, 2019).

9. Bobby Herrera, *The Gift of Struggle: Life-Changing Lessons about
Leading* (Austin, TX: Bard Press, 2019).

Chapter 11

1. Seth Godin, "Let's Stop Calling Them 'Soft Skills,'" *It's Your Turn*
(blog), January 31, 2017, itsyourturnblog.com/lets-stop-calling-them-soft
-skills-9cc27ec09ecb.

2. Jonathan Keyser, "The Anatomy of a Selfless Service Leader with
Jonathan Keyser," interview by Nate Regier, in *On Compassion with Dr. Nate*,
podcast, January 1, 2023, oncompassion.libsyn.com/the-anatomy-of-a
-selfless-service-leader-with-jonathan-keyser.

3. Jonathan Keyser, *You Don't Have to Be Ruthless to Win: The Art of
Badass Selfless Service* (Los Angeles: Lonecrest Publications, 2019).

4. Amy Balog, "Escaping the Purgatory of Middle Management with
Amy Balog," interview by Nate Regier, in *On Compassion with Dr. Nate*,
podcast, November 1, 2022, oncompassion.libsyn.com/the-middle
-managers-struggle-feeling-stuck-and-overloaded-with-amy-balog.

5. Brené Brown, *Atlas of the Heart: Mapping Meaningful Connection and the Language of Human Experience* (New York: Random House, 2021).

6. Keyser, "Anatomy of a Selfless Service Leader."

Chapter 12

1. Scott Shute, "Operationalizing Compassion with Scott Shute," interview by Nate Regier, in *On Compassion with Dr. Nate*, podcast, May 1, 2021, oncompassion.libsyn.com/operationalizing-compassion-with-scott-shute.

2. Silvia Garcia, "Leading with Happiness with Silvia Garcia," interview by Nate Regier, in *On Compassion with Dr. Nate*, podcast, March 1, 2021, oncompassion.libsyn.com/reasons-to-believe-building-happiness-at-coca-cola-with-sylvia-garcia.

3. Laurel Donnellan, "Compassionate Leaders with Laurel Donnellan," interview by Nate Regier, in *On Compassion with Dr. Nate*, podcast, September 1, 2020, oncompassion.libsyn.com/compassionate-leaders-with-laurel-donnellan.

4. Stephen Trzeciak and Anthony Mazzarelli, *Compassionomics: The Revolutionary Scientific Evidence That Caring Makes a Difference* (Pensacola, FL: Studer Group, 2019).

5. Lynne Shallcross, "Who's Taking Care of Superman?" *Counseling Today* (blog), American Counseling Association, January 1, 2013, ct.counseling.org/2013/01/whos-taking-care-of-superman/.

6. Nate Regier, *Conflict without Casualties: A Field Guide for Leading with Compassionate Accountability* (Oakland, CA: Berrett-Koehler, 2017).

7. Dan Rockwell, "Humility as a Group of Practices with Dan Rockwell," interview by Nate Regier, in *On Compassion with Dr. Nate*, podcast, September 1, 2022, oncompassion.libsyn.com/humility-as-a-group-of-practices-with-dan-rockwell.

8. Jill Chang, *Quiet Is a Superpower: The Secret Strengths of Introverts in the Workplace* (Oakland, CA: Berrett-Koehler, 2020); "About Me," Susan Cain, accessed January 20, 2023, susancain.net/about/.

9. Gloria Cotton, "A Blend of Compassion and Accountability with Gloria Cotton," interview by Nate Regier, in *On Compassion with Dr. Nate*, podcast, August 1, 2021, oncompassion.libsyn.com/a-blend-of-compassion -and-accountability-with-gloria-cotton.

Chapter 13

1. Helen Reiss et al., "Empathy Training for Resident Physicians: A Randomized Controlled Trial of a Neuroscience-Informed Curriculum," *Journal of General Internal Medicine* 27, no. 10 (October 2012): 1280–1286.

2. Linda A. Fogarty et al., "Can 40 Seconds of Compassion Reduce Patient Anxiety?" *Journal of Clinical Oncology* 17, no. 1 (January 1999): 371–379.

3. James D. Kirkpatrick and Wendy Kayser Kirkpatrick, *Kirkpatrick's Four Levels of Training Evaluation* (Alexandria, VA: Association for Talent Development, 2016).

4. Tom Kolditz, "Improving Leadership Development Programs with Tom Kolditz," interview by Nate Regier, in *On Compassion with Dr. Nate*, podcast, April 1, 2021, oncompassion.libsyn.com/improving-leadership -development-programs-with-tom-kolditz; Tom Kolditz, Libby Gill, and Ryan P. Brown, *Leadership Reckoning: Can Higher Education Develop the Leaders We Need?* (Oklahoma City: Monocle Press, 2021).

5. Carol Dweck, *Mindset: The New Psychology of Success* (New York: Ballantine, 2007).

INDEX

ABOUT THE AUTHOR

 NATE REGIER, PhD, is the CEO and founder of Next Element, a global culture consulting firm dedicated to bringing more compassion to every workplace. A former practicing clinical psychologist, Nate has deep expertise in behavioral psychology and assessment, social and emotional intelligence and leadership, adaptive communication, conflict communication, and ways to build thriving workplace cultures. He was integral in the development of Next Element's Leading Out of Drama and Compassion Mindset leader development frameworks. He is a certifying master trainer in the Process Communication Model, where his role includes helping with certification and model fidelity around the world.

Nate is a thought leader in the field of compassionate cultures, compassionate conflict, and compassionate communication. He has published three other books on these topics; *Beyond Drama: Transcending Energy Vampires, Conflict without Casualties: A Field Guide for Leading with Compassionate Accountability,* and *Seeing People Through: Unleash Your Leadership Potential with the Process Communication Model.* He is a sought-after keynote speaker, publishes a weekly blog, hosts a podcast, *On Compassion with Dr. Nate,* regularly contributes to industry publications, and appears as a guest on numerous podcasts.

Nate has been married to Julie for twenty-nine years. They have three daughters and are newly minted empty nesters. Nate and Julie live in Newton, Kansas, with their loyal border collie, Milo.

ABOUT NEXT ELEMENT

NEXT ELEMENT is a global consulting firm helping organizations create cultures of Compassionate Accountability so they can thrive in complex and challenging environments. We serve clients of all sizes, from small businesses to multinational corporations, throughout the world.

Compassionate Accountability® is the unifying framework for everything we do. Our reputation for helping clients achieve positive results is grounded in a commitment to model the philosophy and tools we teach. Using scientifically proven assessments and diagnostics, a powerful suite of leader development tools, and a zealous commitment to practical application, our clients empower themselves and their organizations to thrive.

Sustainability and empowerment are the keys to long-term success. In addition to delivering assessment, consulting, and training and coaching programs for our clients, we certify, license, and support others to deliver our curriculum. We have a robust global network of over 120 certified professionals in fourteen countries that work independently as well as inside their organizations to bring Compassionate Accountability to more people each day. Next Element is a US distributor for the Process Communication Model and the owner and worldwide distributor of Leading Out of Drama® and the Compassion Mindset® frameworks.

Next Element is here to help you build your culture of Compassionate Accountability. Visit us at Next-element.com or reach out to info@next-element.com to learn more.

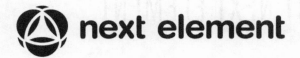

Berrett–Koehler
Publishers

Berrett-Koehler is an independent publisher dedicated to an ambitious mission: *Connecting people and ideas to create a world that works for all.*

Our publications span many formats, including print, digital, audio, and video. We also offer online resources, training, and gatherings. And we will continue expanding our products and services to advance our mission.

We believe that the solutions to the world's problems will come from all of us, working at all levels: in our society, in our organizations, and in our own lives. Our publications and resources offer pathways to creating a more just, equitable, and sustainable society. They help people make their organizations more humane, democratic, diverse, and effective (and we don't think there's any contradiction there). And they guide people in creating positive change in their own lives and aligning their personal practices with their aspirations for a better world.

And we strive to practice what we preach through what we call "The BK Way." At the core of this approach is *stewardship,* a deep sense of responsibility to administer the company for the benefit of all of our stakeholder groups, including authors, customers, employees, investors, service providers, sales partners, and the communities and environment around us. Everything we do is built around stewardship and our other core values of *quality, partnership, inclusion,* and *sustainability.*

This is why Berrett-Koehler is the first book publishing company to be both a B Corporation (a rigorous certification) and a benefit corporation (a for-profit legal status), which together require us to adhere to the highest standards for corporate, social, and environmental performance. And it is why we have instituted many pioneering practices (which you can learn about at www.bkconnection.com), including the Berrett-Koehler Constitution, the Bill of Rights and Responsibilities for BK Authors, and our unique Author Days.

We are grateful to our readers, authors, and other friends who are supporting our mission. We ask you to share with us examples of how BK publications and resources are making a difference in your lives, organizations, and communities at www.bkconnection.com/impact.

Dear reader,

Thank you for picking up this book and welcome to the worldwide BK community! You're joining a special group of people who have come together to create positive change in their lives, organizations, and communities.

What's BK all about?

Our mission is to connect people and ideas to create a world that works for all.

Why? Our communities, organizations, and lives get bogged down by old paradigms of self-interest, exclusion, hierarchy, and privilege. But we believe that can change. That's why we seek the leading experts on these challenges—and share their actionable ideas with you.

A welcome gift

To help you get started, we'd like to offer you a **free copy** of one of our bestselling ebooks:

www.bkconnection.com/welcome

When you claim your **free ebook**, you'll also be subscribed to our blog.

Our freshest insights

Access the best new tools and ideas for leaders at all levels on our blog at ideas.bkconnection.com.

Sincerely,

Your friends at Berrett-Koehler

Certified

Corporation